ACROSS MIRAGE OF LIFE

VOLUME I

SATHEESAN RANGORATH

INDIA • SINGAPORE • MALAYSIA

ISBN 979-8-89026-751-1

Contents

Foreword

My friend Satheesan Rangorath is an earnest writer of poetry in both English and Malayalam. That he has already published a mega volume of 3000 odd poems couple of years back is a testimony of his deep routed interest in expressing his opinions, reactions and intuitive experiences in verse. I am reminded of the famous words of William Blake, "To see a world in a grain *of sand and heaven in a wildflower; Hold infinity in the palm of your hand and eternity in an hour.*" He has been part of few international poetry forums where he had been sharing his poems in English, most of them have brought him ecstatic appreciation and most of them have been grouped under top billings of gold, silver, emerald etc. An essential precondition for being able to appreciate the expression of a poet, is to have an open mind of a virtually blank sheet of white paper. Spontaneous reaction and appreciation arises from this point of view, the international forum of poems must have found the import of the original eastern thoughts and expression of Satheesan to their liking.

Satheesan was in deep love with his beloved wife for nearly 5 decades, emphasises the outlook of a person who sees and values of life in their true shades. It then follows that he has penned many of his poems in the light of their mutual love and bonding. The sad demise of his wife Saroja two years back has left him in a pall of gloom although the spiritual strength that he derives from his guru Matha AmrithanathaMayi (Amma) has been sustaining him in the right spirit.

It may not be possible to take a tour of the 100s of poems that he has penned to review critically, though most of them deserve a look up. One striking feature is however is his infinite attachment to his departed wife that keeps surfacing from his memories and over runs the flow of other inspiring subjects. A rare outpour that strikes as over whelming is when he says, "Each letter was carved from the depth of my thoughts, erected a mansion adorned with selected artefacts Don't know when you will find it, may be trade wings carry it up to you ………………………." and the flow of his thoughts continues with equal depth". The depth of his pain while featuring the war-torn areas of Ukraine, the focus is on the Ambarnaya river which he paints as strips in red what with the massive oil pollution, "She is just a young girl turned into puberty…… they deflowered her near the Russian city of Norilsk in Siberia". The reflection of his subtle meditative observation of his Guru Matha Amritananta Mayi, he expresses his experience thus, "once she said; in the end, there is nothing but a bit smile, end of knowledge and beginning of wisdom". The smile is beatific, decidedly. His imagination runs wild and captures a thought of a "Thanksgiving theme" where he pens thus; "he had oceaning dreams, life swam in the water. Birds land over the sea, fishes become foods for birds. Giant monster land over the earth".

A humorous fling on business channels where 'breaking news' of these channels has become the order of the day; he brands them as armchair journalism thinning out into the yellow media. He paints it little more vividly when he says "Often the judges that deliver judgments kill and create celebrities, the thief becomes a saint and the saint becomes a thief." Under the caption 'great barrier reef' his paint brush takes a meaningful swipe across the canvas when he says, "A heritage hiding in the Coral Sea meditating in the severity, silent chanting .....Dreaming in the paradise lost" In a subtler take on "aromatic autumn", he says "dreams hibernate, opening of fresh pink faces sprouts......how do I catch the picture of this exotic painting....." Reflecting his thoughts under the caption 'Android dream' the thoughts takes an imaginative run at a speed that mind only can generate, 'Suddenly my android lands on a bumpy ramp....................... Gliding like a fashion model placing a footprint on the martian land spraying and playing holi colours. About the ownership of this earth, he sketches with his pen painfully reflecting on the wars and consequential effect of slavery and wide spread damage to the peace lovers and closes with a helpless tail-peace with prophetic words, "One day you will have a shock, a cultural shock............in the annals of history you live as arsonists and extortionists, war mongers of modernity".

Satheesan is a serious thinker and reacts inwardly to situations in life although being a non-controversial person that he is, his impressions often find expression in words in his poems. The topics that bear out of this attribute cover a wide range of common day situations as political, social personal, interpersonal, cultural and spiritual. "I do not know what I am looking for with along tickling tongue. May be an entry to your soul I, have my tongue print on you as an id card". Or for that matter he writes in one instance, "when I write a poem it's a dream come true: from the silence of the mind, from the deep slumber of thoughts I discover a word, an image, or a soul full feeling of glitter." This should reveal the pen picture of a poet who finds expression of his thoughts and impressions of the world through poems, an average of more than one per day. He is on the eve of releasing his latest volume of poems of few thousands. I wish him all the best and may he continue to inspire and impress the world of poetry lovers for a long time to come.

– **Brig Narayan Menon (Retd)**

May I present this anthology of my poems with humility before the reading intelligentsia Many of these poems are participants in various competitions conducted by a US-based poetry site named Allpoetry.com. There are five categorised sections according to the medals they won from the competition as Gold, Silver, Bronze and Emerald. A few are under general categories which were applauded by the host. However, I am leaving it to the reader (if any!) to judge.

We were rowing our boat together in troubled waters. The river flooded several times rocking our raft severely yet, we managed the rudder steady and kept the mast adjusted to the flow of wind. The river was streaming at the high spate.

Somewhere beyond the time we travelled to the time and dived through many lives, discarded our clothes many times. Carried carryovers of Karma from previous births, the burden was heavy, the sack was full.

At a different point in time, we were born. Destiny united us in human life as husband and wife. We were bound together with wedlock. Since then, we had our happy moments, good times, and bad times. It was also our fate that had forbidden us from having more attachments as our children. Me and Saru (Saroja) and accepted the reality we became a child to each other and looked after well. Time took out us to different scenes and scenarios. We could adjust mutually to the hard facts of life.

However, no complaints we respected each other, and I was not an overbearing husband. She was gentle and cute and approved of all my decisions. All her suggestions were honoured in our day-to-day life.

I was having a good bank job in the United Arab Emirates. Greed did not attack us. My job was enough for both of us and our future family. We decided to be peaceful at home having only one earning member. I met all her desires and commitments without any grumbling. The purse was common. She hardly had any requirements. Even jewellery and comforts were all reasonable and judged. She had an aversion for show and display, which she might have imbibed from my character. We were happy and had our fights too.

Life took us to different modes. Like any newly married we desired to have our kids. However, we realised the reality after 12 years of treatment often visits to infertility clinics. Frustration and pressure gave us a down spirit after the abortion of the first pregnancy. Again continuing the treatment was depressing and traumatic for her. We decided not to and decided to return home. I was in my 50s and Saroja was 40. We settled in Palakkad without any regrets. Shortly after she was ill with a compressed disc problem. Bedridden for 3 months. from there onwards, our struggle with diseases started ending up with a Renal problem. The treatment continued for 18 years. In the meantime, I had to undergo bypass surgery and a carsova of bladder problems.

Despite all, we had our good times too. Proudly I can say I took her to many countries as a tourist. We visited Abu Dhabi, Dubai, my former place of employment. Then to Singapore and Malaysia. The land of wonders placed our footprints at Change international airport. Singapore. Visiting Marina Singapore giant wheel gave us a lasting impression of the city. Touching the feet of Lord Muruga we visited the Batu cave in Malaysia and then to Genting heights where we put our feet in the largest hotel in the world First World Hotel. Birds park, orchid garden. We returned to India with a long-lasting impression and a craving for more travel.

Next year we took a vacation to Europe, starting from London, A historic city on the banks of the Thames river, the Land of merchants and political feuds. A country of great writers, scholars, and world-famous universities. A city associated with Indian leaders like Gandhi and Nehru. Unforgettable London eye on the banks of river Thames. Smooth streaming river filled with Cruise ships and boats. Several overhead bridges connecting both banks are littered with historical buildings. we had a memorable cruise on the river. We witnessed Big ben, parliament house, and Westminster Abbey. Buckingham palace. Overnight cruise to the Netherlands world's Tulip garden, Rotterdam, Amsterdam, and Hague. Our bus was waiting to take us to the selected European countries. Belgium chocolate street, artificial diamonds, Austria <u>zavrouski crystals</u> showroom. In Austria, we stayed in a 400-year-old wooden hotel. We're living through history. Liechtenstein, a small country between Austria and Switzerland memory ligers, we shopped for a small memento, a collapsible cup, which Saroja kept in her bag handy. Through the tunnels of Alphs, we reached France. The ancient beautiful city of Paris, the city of lights, the Eifel tower, intricate architecture flawless engineering. My wife bought some scarves of silk from the hawkers near the tower as a souvenir for our Paris visit. Placed a rose on the under path where Princess Diana had her last trip. Most photographed Élysée Palace, palace and garden. the seine river cruise was another milestone in memory lane. Again our bus took us to Italy. The first city we visited was Florence. The city of painters and artisans.

Great. Leonardo Davinci and Michelangelo, of Italy We paid our silent respects to these renowned masters. Venice is a wonderful piece of heaven on earth." Ponte delle Guglie, Ponte dei Tre Archi is unique among the bridges of Venice for its design; there used to be a few other three-arched bridges in the city, but this is the only one that has survived to this day. 11. Ponte dei Bareteri" Most Famous Bridges in Venice Bridge of Sighs. This infamous footbridge connects the Doge's Palace with the Prigioni (prisons). Though many visitors... Rialto Bridge. Glass blower's gallery took us by surprise. Very exquisite display of vases and other artefacts Salutations to those artisans. The Vatican is another small city-state. RevH.H Pope Francis was on rounds in his pope mobile. We visited the Sistine chapel.

Thrilled to see the ceiling paintings of Davinci In 2018 we took another tour of the Peoples Republic Of China, Hong Kong and Macau. We visited the forbidden city of Royalty, the Temple of Heaven, and the Doomed silence of Tianmin square. Sounds of the Bootfall of soldiers, the helpless cry of students who fought for freedom daringly. There Saroja had a lasting memory. She endured and walked the entire parade ground about two KM or more barefooted. Her slipper strap had broken there were no shops in that area she took it sportingly and walked through. Even she made a friendship with a janitor woman and secured herself an old sandal for the rest of the city round tour. She kept it as a souvenir after coming back. The memories of the great wall of china and the pride we could reach there, from the words of high school history books. The fast-growing shanghai city is a very picturesque modern city, we visited the shanghai tower and had a bird's eye view of the city. The Everlasting experience of bullet train rides The 1931km high-speed railway links Shanghai and Hong Kong. There is only one high-speed train G99 from Shanghai Hongqiao Railway Station to Hong Kong West Kowloon Railway Station at 02:10 PM every day. The duration is 8 hours and 18 minutes.

In Hong Kong, the remarkable visit was to Victoria Peak The peak tram is a funicular railway in Hong Kong, which carries both tourists and residents to the upper levels of Hong Kong Island. Running from Garden Road Admiralty to Victoria Peak via the Mid-Levels, it provides the most direct route and offers good views over the harbour and skyscrapers of Hong Kong. Hydrofoil ferry takes you to Macau in 45 mins. The land of casinos and 7-star hotels

All these travel notes I am writing to say that it was a great achievement for me and Saroja. despite our illness, I had bypass surgery and Saroja's deteriorating kidney disease was a challenge for both of us. In the previous paragraph, I forgot to add Saroja could travel in a cable car to Mount Titlis in Switzerland where the temperature was -20 celsius at that time. I made an Ice idol of Lord Ganesh. On the Ice hill.

Next year we took out vacation to Australia.. while floating in a hot air balloon In Cairnes We were scaling a negative mind to positivity. We got our first hot air ballooning certificate from Australia.

While rowing through the dark caves of glow worms we achieved another remarkable experience of fantasy. A speed boat ride was another adventure that I took to Saroja in New Zealand. The thrill was that I did not tell her that we were going on an adventure cruise. She was surprised that she had gone through the ride courageously.

There are many experiences to write about, but this is just a writeup of words built on the tomb of my wife, a " Taj Mahal of

Jade". I erect this Sculpture of words in the unvisited celestial garden in my heart and soul.

I don't know I lost. Still, my chest heaves her breathe last sound of pumping feeble with her moan. A short whisper strained whistling nostrils, parting grief, eyes wide a silent trickle of pain unable to hear her gestures to console. My legs faltered fear consumed poring cold sweat shivering shaking hands and legs. On my lap, she rested her head her last.....grip

I was helpless and did not have the penance to go behind Yamadharma Raja. I am not Nachiketa to follow Yama to Dharma Puri in order to get Saroja out. No one heard my cry at the odd hour of that black dawn. complete silence, my teardrops frozen Still, Now I am crying silently on my lonely nights and stillness of dawn every day calling the names of the lord.

These words in the poetry collection are my respectful homage to my wife Saroja. Probably the writings of an insignificant Pen to an unknown person. After all who will remember my wife after my departure? There is no hope of anyone doing any annual Balikarma for us. This is an epithet on the tomb of two unknown individuals who visited this earth for a short time and returned to infinity.

In the loneliness we used to watch the sunrise and diving sun together. She left yesterday leaving me alone and aloof. When this long wait will end?

Left me alone saw it all closing of a dream curtain down, we were talking about plans for dialysis, transplant, and donors, for my further... suddenly my breath stopped eyes were half closed am I in a psychedelic vision panicky sounds dressed to the hospital siren of an ambulance hopeful blue beacon light She was holding my hands pressing the chest to straighten, collapsed hands, dangling neck, sweat on forehead wiped by a hairy hand, breath stopped one inhalation and the last exhalation. Moon just disappeared leaving black clouds an owl busily turned his head and fluttered away into the darkness. Helpless shouts, cries, helpless sighs my dear I gave her resuscitation sprinkled with cold water yet, she had reached another world of brilliance left me alone.

A Passionate hug A passionate hug, I hear your heart, Your heartbeat, the chirp of your soul. Lovebird sings. I hear mine too. Through soft music, song of souls. Lovebirds sing. Together we hear the Symphony of millions, the music of souls. Echo of spirits, Deep in and out, vibrate in rhythm, love boundless. In the ocean of love, One with the cosmos, We merge in every atom, one soul; one song. I embrace, merging in oneness. I breathe in Breathe out. Turning into a dream, I fly high, and as I float, my wings cover the entire universe. We disappear In subtle softness. When you call I reverberate, from silence world around reply to my wish! End my monologue

I PLACE MY FLOWERS OF WORDS AT THE FEET OF MY BELOVED SAROJA, THE LOTUS

Pranamam

Aum Amriteswaryei Namaha

Pranam to my beloved Guru H.H. Mata Amritanandamayi Devi, She is my inspiration and Muse Saraswathi Devi

Aum Namashivaya.

Satheesan Rangorath

Dedication

I dedicate this collection ACROSS MIRAGE OF LIFE in loving memory of my departed wife Saroja Satheesh (Saru). She had helped me come through many hard times while she was succumbing to fate. May this Taj Mahal of words be a mausoleum created by an unknown person to an unknown person.

Born to parents M. Sreedharan Nair, and Sarada Amma, Satheesan Rangorath completed his early education in the schools of his village, Elappulli in Palakkad District of Kerala, India. He graduated in Commerce from the Government Victoria College Palakkad. About this time he migrated to Bombay in search of a job, a feature common to many youngsters in those days. This is a looking back to the Path he trekked from 19/Nov/1948. As a simple observer of life, he has said many interesting things in simple vocabulary. His poems are not complicated and readable to any layman, who has basic knowledge of English. Quiet and generally reserved from his early days, he had found the power of poetry as a profoundly satisfying form of expression in a world that cannot stop talking. His intuitive response to the varieties of life situations interwoven with the mysteries of mother nature has aided the creative flow from within, helping himself to ink the lines in his leisure hours as a routine from his youth.

He graduated in law in 1978 before he moved to the United Arab Emirates where he served as a bank officer for 27 years. Supporting him in all walks of life has been his beloved wife, Saroja, a soft-spoken and able homemaker. In the year 2021 December 19, she left her heavenly abode. And this collection of his poem" ACROSS MAIRAGE OF LIFE IS" HIS HOMAGE AND DEDICATION IN MEMORY OF HIS BELOVED WIFE. Satheesan Rangorath has published his poems in many poetry forums and has received several accolades. " MEMORY SPROUTS" VOL I, II AND III his SECOND Publication. found entry into record books, India Book Of Records and Asia book of Records in the year. SNAPSHOTS OF A FIREFLY was his first published work of poems.

It is a huge collection of poems painted on a vast canvas. His bristly strokes are." Across mirage of life" is his third publication a poetry Mausoleum in memory of his wife Saroja Satheesh become a signature of his soulful vision across mirage of life.

Barbie Dolls

In my dreams,

I play with Gods.

They are my Barbie dolls.

They guard me,

When dawn arrives.

They are my food,

When my dad sells them

As a package deal.

They sit in the hearts

And become food,

For thoughts.

Her last

I don't know I lost...
still, my chest heaves her breathe
last sound of pumping
feeble with her moan
a short whisper
short whistling nostrils

parting grief eyes wide
a silent trickle of pain
unable to hear me
her gestures to console

my legs faltered
fear consumed
poring cold sweat
shivering shaking hands and legs

on my lap
she rested her head
her last.....grip

She left * * *

I heard owls hoot

hoo hoo hoo hooo

black moon gliding

street dogs howling

we talked about love in hushed tones

fear struck eyes bulged

breathed slowly sipping scanty air

parting breathing fewer lips

built a vacuum around her

the voice struck my throat

did not hear me

my panicky prayers

fear vibes

dried my throat

no one heard my screaming

one last look

tried to breathe into her lungs

a soft kiss

her hands cascaded down

collapsed

necks tilting like babies

closed her eyes

the half-opened mouth

she left

my dry tears on her lips

no one heard me

I was helpless

no one.........

My wife left to infinity

to the hands of Providence

grieved parched lips

Memoirs

Tickling glowworms awakened

from the deep dormancy

your soft petal lips moved on my body

a thousand centipedes creeping

invoking prurient cells of my brain

we were afloat in a lotus boat

rolling in a whirlpool of exciting desires

exploring underneath our sensual emotional pool

we embraced our bodies tight

bubbling and nibbling our tongues

I watched silver beads drizzling off your wet long hair

under the moonlit, we saw our glow

dancing in a pool of enlightenment

finally sleeping on a heaving water bed

you were a dream in my secret casket

where I had you invoked in a rosebud

often awakening you in my glittering memoir

Loneliness

We used to watch

the sunrise

and diving sun together

she left yesterday

leaving me alone aloof

when this long wait

will loneliness end?

Left me be alone

Saw it all

closing of a dream

curtain down

we were talking about plans

dialysis

transplant

donors for my furthermore

suddenly

my breath stopped

eyes half closed

am I in a psychedelic vision

panicky sounds

dressed to hospital

siren of ambulance

hopeful blue beacon light

he was holding my hands

pressing the chest

straightened collapsed hands
dangling neck

sweat on forehead
wiped by a hairy hand
breath stopped
one inhalation
and the last exhalation

moon just disappeared
leaving black clouds
an owl busily turned his head
fluttered away into the darkness

helpless shouts
cry
helpless sighs
my dear
I gave her resuscitation
sprinkled cold water
yet
she had reached another world
of brilliance
left me alone

A Passionate hug

A passionate hug,

I hear your heart,

Your heartbeat,

the chirp of your soul.

Lovebird sings.

I hear mine too.

Through soft music,

song of souls.

Lovebirds sing.

Together we hear,

Symphony of millions,

music of souls.

Echo of spirits,

Deep in and out,

vibrate in rhythm,

love boundless.

In the ocean of love,

One with cosmos,

We merge in every atom,

one soul; one song.

I embrace,

merging in oneness.

I breathe in

Breathe out.

Turning into a dream,

I fly high, and as I float,

wings cover,

entire universe.

We disappear

In subtle softness.

When you call

I reverberate,

form silence

world around

reply to my wish!

End my monologue

You left suddenly and walked out in a huff

closing all windows and doors

my window with a view is blocked

skyscrapers sprung around

obstructing sun and moonlight

stars used to peep into our bedroom

pouring blue lights

pieces of snow clouds visited us

our dreams were colourful

like the dancing butterflies

during spring season

I loved watching your dark blue hair

flutter behind your neck

your moonlit blossoms

your booms shine

depth of your dimples, slightly parted lips

made me dive into you

explore fathoms of inner currents

we flew over

above the magic lands

fantasy islands where we nested

our dreams

erected magic arch of a rainbow

weaved many silky thoughts together

yet, you left dumping our home

into the hands of loneliness

making a dustbin

still, I wait for you

for the memorable day

you arrive to light the fire

spread the warmth of your laughter

your giggle, smile

let us light that oil wick

in the brass sacred lamp

I am tired of soliloquy

end my monologue, Please

I am here alone

The panic button was pressed in my composure

she was breathing heavily while consoling me

I ran shouting weeping screaming fear vibes

ran madly to my neighbourhood at 3 am

help help help

back and forth to see how she was doing

I found her collapsed neck and hands touching deadline last
sound of breath

resuscitation attempts failed in my helplessness

kissed her breathing to revive her

no, she left with a smile on her eyes

holding my neck desperately departed

still, I am holding a half-bloomed rose

I listen to her love beats

Sediments of time

leftover daylight

giant darkness spread his wings

streaked trees display

autumnal breeze

embraces the first winter night

the murmur of cold winds

first snowflakes

flutter around the valley

I cover my face with a blanket

sleep hugs me tight to her warm breasts

lullaby

I listen to her love beats

A woman completes a man

I do not know you

Because I am a man

yet I know you in my heart

as a subtle soft silky petal

that keeps me upright

I respect you

there is an intricate

unattainable part in you

secured fastened sect

that is mystery

nobody can decode it

it is your secret

a grey area fogged

flagged and fastened

by a combination lock

secret password

gets erased with her departure!

But I know you

a decent righteous woman

plays a great part in life

merges with man

and fulfils

tidiness of race

a woman completes a man

a man completes a woman

Across mirage of life

Lost out at sea on my only boat

in my panic, I went and lost its only oar'

my head was reeling

the country boat was circling in the unknown directions

Regaining senses and awareness of reality

stopped pressing the panic button

into the serene sea, a slow wind blows

my boat slowly started drifting

took a quick look at my ration, the water bottle was half
empty

few pieces of bread and a little jam left

on review of the situation, I decided to survive

my fishing line is intact

removed my red T-shirt

hoisted as an alert flag

safely kept away the matchbox

lied flat on my back

feeling the turbulence of the sea

waves clatter on my raft

have to move in the east direction

decided to leave it to a destiny where it takes me

as floated in the current out of the world

watched small fishes move around me

my flag was flying high like a mast

dreamt about 'the old man and sea'

Skelton of my thoughts

life is a journey across

crossing the ocean of life to the shore

where the reality of life after

in a fisherman's net, the smart fish escape

others get entangled in the cruel fate

hope someone finds me before darkness consumes my
rudderless ship!

let miracles happen in the mirages of life

waiting for the sight of an Oasis!

Days have gone like seconds

Days have gone like seconds

since we had our pink hearts pierced

with a flower arrow of cupid ten years back

our nuptial bliss remains blooming

your countenance behind the veil of shyness where I saw a
unique expression

from the births and rebirths, we lived together like a folding
unfolding dream

still, I remember the wedding day

with your half bloom smile of a flower

sparkling in the exquisite wedding sari

brocaded in sacred threads on intimacy

all moments we spent together

were divine with enchanting colours

some times we quarrelled for nothing

only to reinforce our care for each other

I remember the motherly smile on your face

when our baby girl was born

seasons passed through ten years

like day dreamer I remain

Wings Inside

Serenity flows off heaven.

Smooth stream full of love.

Lifting the veil of mystery,

Divinity peeps out.

The charisma of nature reflects,

On a lake of tranquillity.

A divine symphony is created.

Rhythmic silence hangs.

The meditative mind merges.

Becomes one with the fly.

A flutter of wings inside.

Love doves fly to freedom.

Remain Puny

I caricatured life

in my hands

with its full

colour and splendour.

I remain puny

Colours I mixed

The most beautiful feeling of life

Unfolds before me as a woman in love.

You are a creation from the

Sweetest of my imagination

Came live through the stretches of my thoughts.

You lived in my heart for a long time,

Tickling my senses teasingly

In your warmth, I spent my lonely nights

Embraced your softness crushing you

Tight to my chest every night.

You smeared your collyrium on my face.

I cherished your lip marks in my mind

and a shade of vermilion on my chest.

I made you the heroine in my fantasy

and we scaled the heights of heaven.

When I slept tired I knew your anxiety,
Watching me closely; breathing heavily.
One day I had to present you to the world.
Slowly I invoked you in sketches
Put you on an easel of my vision
Painted in oil colours I mixed specially for you.

I adored your nude with my passion
Ornamented your femininity with love.
I put my face of respect on your body
kissing and fomenting each cell.
painted you in my canvas as a heritage
Of female beauty ever discovered by a man

Flower gets admired in the presence of beetles
beetle gets noticed when the flowers bloom
in his heart, tickling.
Love percolates spread fragrance.
My painting completes with a brushstroke of my passion

An attempt (Bussokusekika style)
We are born in a dream

sleepwalking into unknown

stepping on rough rocks

wading on the ink of darkness

we move at a slow pace ashore

there we join the sunbathers

Author notes:

Number of Syllables: 38

Words with syllables counted programmatically: N/A

Words: 28

Characters

(all | no spaces | with spaces): 211 | 126 | 155 (Sequential spaces are not counted)

Lines: 6 (Including empty lines)

Letters (number of each): There are 8 a's. There are 2 b's. There are 2 c's. There are 3 ds. There are 16s. There are 1 f's. There are 4 g's. There are 5 hs. There are 8 i's. There are 1 j's. There are 5 k's. There are 3 l's. There are 2 m's. There are 16s. There are 12s. There are 4 p's. There are 9 rs. There are 9 s's. There are 5 t's. There are 3 u's. There are 1 v's. There are 7 w's.

Pygmalion effect

Between light and shades

I created an image of curves

shaded you with unique hues.

my eyes opened to your nudity

filling every bit of your body

with pixels of perfection

I made you pose explicit

yours became a feast for my camera

we communicated with you

filling you with hopes of

a pinup girl centre spread

I carved out your womanhood

my flash embossed your booms

and depressions to aesthetics

then I breathed love and life

to fill you with a Pygmalion effect

We forget to live

Magnificent five explored the world

they saw the wonders of this planet

had their eyes wide open

met with exotic creation and beauty

listened to the birds sing sweet songs

the fresh fragrance of flowers they breathe

played with colourful butterflies

followed them to find their homes

bathed in the warmth of the sun

kept their senses wide open

then came the reward of the day

the whistle of the ice cream man

each secured their favourite flavours

enjoying every bit of the pleasure

Kids live from moment to moment

tasting life in its fullness

we adults sit before a cup of delicacy

but never eat it in time, before,

life gets melted with the obvious. we forget to live.

Ettu Brute

When M.K. Gandhi was booted out

by a British official

from a first-class compartment of a train

to Pretoria in South Africa,

the modern history of India begins.

Seeds for the independence struggle

were planted unaware in his mind.

Mohandas Karamchand Gandhi,

a fashionable well-groomed young barrister

from the temple of law, University College, London became

a renunciant and the greatest revolutionary

that world has ever produced.

Armed with a Bible in one hand and Gita

in another hand, he went out to fight British Empire.

His strongest weapon was nonviolence

and starvation; he did that successfully

in achieving his goal of dehoisting Union Jack.

After spending twenty-one years in South Africa

his motherland was calling him for his leadership.

Nationalism and patriotism had rooted in the Indian mind.

The intelligentsia had grouped them.

There was a lack of united leadership.

On arrival in Bombay Gandhi met all the great leaders

LalPalBal, Gokhele, Patel, Mothilal Nehru

Chitharanjan Das, Rajaji, Dr. Rajendraparsad, sarojini Naidu

Gobindballab pant, Subash chandrabose

Pundit Jawaharlal Nehru, Mohammed Ali Jinnah,

and many more leaders were at the forefront.

All of them were unique in many ways

in thoughts, actions and idealism they all joined

hands with Mahatma Gandhi.

More than that, Gandhi entered into the very hearts of

Indians and planted the seeds for Indian Nationalism, freedom

Truth, equality and fraternity were his preachings.

He lit a candle of love and awakened people from all walks of
life

for freedom struggle.

In the process Jawaharlal Nehru son of Motilal Nehru

became his darling,

an ardent follower of Mahatma Gandhi.

Naturally, other leaders equally loved

by Mr Gandhi, one among was Sardar Vallabhai Patel,

Rajendra Prasad and Mohammaed Ali Jinnah were

also found a place in Gandhiji's heart

one of the most remarkable leaders was

Subhash Chandra Bose who openly questioned

Passive revolution of Gandhi and even won

To become Congress Party president opposing

Gandhiji's nominated candidate for the Presidentship of

Nationalist party.

As for Nehru, there were many rivals,

but he was a darling of Gandhi

He used this advantage to usurp himself into leadership

And became the darling of the masses too.

The major rift in his position came when Jinnah wanted

to be heard as a nationalist Muslim leader,

and he had his ambition; clashing with Nehru's plans.

It was Nehru's wish that turned the table,

and ultimate cessation of Pakistan east and west.

Nehru was an honourable man.

He had a vision and dream for India,

but one cannot say it was in synchronization

with Gandhiji's economic and political policy.

Somehow Nehru convinced Gandhiji of his plans.

In the charisma of his utopian dreams of socialisation

the dreams of Sardar Valla Bhai Patel,

and SubhashChandra'sBose's dreams were flooded out.

We learned a history distorted.

Where we saw the supremacy of one family

That is the family at one Theen Moorthi Bhavan.

Nehru's foreign policy of Non-Alliance was remarkable.

But his economic policy was in the doldrums.

The history we learned was not the real history of India.

They're a big element of manipulation

We never learned the roles of Subhash Chandra Bose,

Or Patel who played a master role in India's freedom struggle.

Of late we hear that Bose was not killed in the so-called plane

Crash. He was living in china or Russia (yet to be clarified
the date of his death)

And his family members were under constant snoop

By Nehru's instance.

While people were made to believe that Bose had died,

Here comes the question.

Who were the hero and villain

Maybe if one can borrow from Shakespeare,

Oh Et tu Brute (Oh you too Brutus)

Author notes:

I am not sure this is a good poem. But I post it as an expression of my thoughts.

No bad intention whatsoever.

5/7/5/ *girls play with Barbie/*

Girls play with Barbie

women play with fantasy

men play with muteness

Chameleon

Hiding behind stimuli,

yet i am a chameleon,

reality unexposed.

When you are one with my soul,

you know the secret of my secrets.

Mother earth's sigh

The burrow of greed

splits the earth

they steal and empty

the bowels

extract metals, minerals

sands, stones even

fertility and water tables

the air is polluted

water contaminated

rivers dry

when nothing remains

they migrate to other planets

mother earth

got time to take a deep sigh

of relief before they come back

for another excavation

Please God

I climb up the mountain to see the heavenly sky

reaching both arms out, and praying to God

asking Him not to pass me by

give me a sign so I can fly

my heart is weak, I need to seek

your amazing grace, please God

help me shed weight

crush my ego, guide me

though turbulence'

am your helpless child

crying for your mercy

take me into your abode

cover me with a blanket

of your wisdom

An attempt in the darkness

Jog with me

see my sweaty prominent curves

jump and dangle rhythmic

No, don't.

Meditate n' Take a deep breath

Bath in the cool golden mist

come to pool

watch me in a new swimsuit

see how I straddle in the pond

my eyes are open

don't see anything

the mind rests in infinity

want you to foam my assets

Come if you care

I am taking a shower

I touch your lusty feelings

With a frost

I am blind to see you hurt

Memorabilia of love

I hide in my thoughts

like a hermit butterfly.

I sing and dance on your body

spraying a mist of heaven

I place my lip mark tattoos

on all over your body

as memorabilia love

Rock Universe

The chair is made of three aspects

Body mind and intellect

directly linked to Ego, illusion and action

once an individual soul meets

supreme soul

all three fingers will

turn into existence, knowledge, and bliss

sit well and rock the universe

Shower of elegance

Let me shower you

with the purity of my thoughts

I love to see you drenched

in the spray of rose water

I watch your body covered

with a wet white silky robe

let me be with you in the cool drizzle

of love

the soft subtle mystic fragrance

cover our bodies

our hands entwine tight

immerse in the worship of bodies

every moment we admire

live under the shower of elegance

slowly we explore

heavenly sweetness

The simile of penance

Life in the world is a gambling den

entangled in the labyrinth of time

fate suffers in the cobweb of Maya*

helpless five senses were shut down

Draupadi the simile of penance,

the uniting force of consciousness

was burned in the fire of sacrifice

Lord adorned her with celestial clothing

*M aya= Illusion

A job well done

Golden wheat field

emits a heavenly hue

a cool breeze makes a wave

bunch of grains shake head

a tune of divine hum pass-through

the poet strolls

over the ridge

a float of fragrant words

dance as floaters

his nostrils wide

greetings the aroma of

idyllic beauty

all works on words

dance before the creator

they do a cosmic dance

in attunement with the rhythm of life

he scribbles a poem

in his mind

and hums it loudly

the song of wheat grains

he(ONV) sang for the down trodden

every word he wrote had a veil

when lifted

soft face of alluring images

zoom in

metaphor and philosophy

flowed in

he cries, smiles

shouts in anger

sometimes he keeps silence

a silence so meaningful

a rain cloud

ready to shower ambrosia

the smell of the first rain

good earth

fresh sprouts come

silky leaves

wave from his pen

he weaves a sonnet

gave life to his thoughts

glanced at each syllable

he infused life

and the golden grains

heaped as a small hill

gets carried away one by one

by ants

he smiles from his heart

tucking pen in his pocket

he returns

a job well done

Holy Holi

The mist of winter still looms

the aroma of fresh air brings nostalgia

time slowly trekked back to another attire

flower buds sprout in every plant and tree

wildflowers started to show up on roadsides

morning sun tickles life to wake up into a colourful world

birds spread their wings into the vastness of the azure sky

every nook and corner is filled with exquisiteness

peasant's granaries are full

they are erecting arches of their happiness

their mind of hopes flies high up in the sky as kites

their colourful thoughts spray colour schemes each other

drenching with love and hopes

intoxicated with the exotic nature

they dance drink and play

joining in the colour burst of nature

from far south I spray a colour jet

erecting a rainbow on earth of my dreams

Strange Beings

With a soul full of words,

mind full of thoughts,

heart full of love,

he was looking for her.

Trekked length and breadth,

by searching eyes.

Wondering where she is?

A bag filled with his loin clothes,

he moved from city to city,

village to village.

Turning himself as seasons

Met many women,

Lived in, cuddled by them.

Figured and hatched by their warmth.

Ultimately he wrote many poems.

Floating himself on a lotus boat,

filling it with petals of his heart,

soft, rose lotus petals.

The emitted fragrance of his love,

sprinkled 'Salt and Pepper'

he left each of his women,

by making a poem of his love.

Intoxicated by unique aroma,

of their body and hair oil.

He wrote divine verses of passion.

Left; leaving a candy box for his children.

Behind waves of exaltation

Barracuda arrived

In a silvery disco costume.

The lights are on,

colourful laser beams flash

with electronic music.

His body is lit with LED.

Dancers float and swim

to the tune of music.

He smiles with wide

open mouth in hope.

He rubs his teeth with fins.

His costume is in the glow

with psychedelic lights.

Holding an imaginative

the guitar he pretended playing

with strings.

Turning and twisting

he started dancing

ecstatically.

The stage was reeling,

many dancers joined him

started rolling along with his steps.

The colour around him turned red.

One by one

all the dancers disappeared.

He was let alone.

Wiping his mouth

he disappeared

behind waves of exaltation.

Balloon Man

Balloon man blowing his balloons,

shaping into different colours n forms.

Every blow is filled with his thoughts,

desires to create creamy dreams.

He sells his bubbles to children,

Invading into their helplessness,

forcing them to part with their meagre cash,

making them feel happy as if holding a treasure.

Soon children burst bubbles,

their cry rises in the air so loud.

But alas, the dream seller disappears,

floating away precariously on a tiny string.

There litter patches of many colours

as if the rainbow had busted out of the sky.

the flesh of clouds scattered lies everywhere,

like human hopes rotting on a hit-and-run.

As a lone ranger balloon man hangs,

holding on to his lone noble thought.

Disintegrated he dissolves into the vastness,

united with the ultimate reality of oneness.

Guide me, Mom

It is a unique chair

kept in my mind,

ornamented

it with classic designs.

I often watched it

with care and reverence.

Offered flowers daily

sprinkled fragrance.

It is a sacred chair

that I will not use.

It is for you Holy Mother

been waiting for you.

Come guide me, Mom

Sound of Music

In the primitive mind

first came

primordial sound ' Aum'

Brain recorded it.

Throat and tongue

repeated it

From one sound

many drizzled

clanging.

Thoughts absorbed

chain of sounds

indifferent tones

each sound was

attributed to an object

The man applied a voice

for a thought,

brain recognized,

applied to an object,

He started

writing alphabets

in picture shapes

Hieroglyphics.

Evolutions,

calligraphy developed.

Close to heart

sounds reverberated

producing

sounds of drumming

Soul started singing

rhythmic melodies

"Ragas" flowed

Divine musical downpour.

Sleeping

in the cradle of music.

Child in you

slept feeding,

nipples of a lullaby.

A sound of music!

The abundance of elegance

The lake lay stretched
extending to serenity.
One sound, a breath
makes a wave on the surface.

As if in a meditation
she keeps a celestial silence.
Like a convex lens
she rolls silently.

The entire universe looks
into her eyes for a makeover.
Azure sky cascades
with the abundance of
elegance.
The indigo seeps into her.
The sun left his

surrealistic pink on her face.
Sometimes she looks
like an intoxicated vampire
thirsty for love.
Her long black hair spread
on the shore.

The entire stars
and the moon descend
to have a closer look
at their excellence.
In a bubble of uncertainty
the entire galaxies
reflects in the lake.

Out of curiosity silvery
fishes jump out
to see what is happening.
Out of nowhere
the sweet melody flows
from a flute,
makes a soft wave of divine

reflection

in the air.

With a meditating mind,

I see the image of

God everywhere.

Mind float in the lake

with a smile of peace.

Line of hope

I walk in the clouds, to see what is behold the silver line

but nothing is there to show me a line

I search and search, but there is no silver line

what do I do when I am out of time

Pleading with time

I sat on a rocky delusion.

Time was smiling, comforting me

with mischief.

I looked among silvery clouds

angels were riding it

I flashed my wish

mind reflected

I was enlightened

with a line of hope

Rolling stone

This journey began aeons back.

A cliff on the mountain slides down

destroying devastating demolishing

uprooting the lives of many people around.

Slowly time changed, and peace dawned

I became a boulder and tumbled down

making a path of destruction for all.

The turn of nature pushed me into a stream

I was rolling on the bed of a speeding river.

my unknown journey started to continue

un-destined.

My life moved along with the flow.

Many terrains came into my vision

meadows, groves, and forests

all this time I was pushed into the current.

I was smoothened in shape and size,

turned into a soft mellow white stone.

Over this period, I became

a stone platform for cloth washers.

A deluge pushed me down to the river again

to continue the journey.

I became a rolling stone moving in the time

I became a part of the stone bed of the river

filtering water to clarity and purity.

My life became a mystery in the flow

from an utter disorder, I flowed into a stream.

My journey had to continue

until I become a grain of sand.

declaring my puny tiny state in the flood of time

fit to be used in a concrete mix.

or maybe I join you on the bed of the ocean.

to be consumed by a rainbow-lipped oyster

to perfect me as an exotic pearl.

"In the end, it's not the years in your life that count. It's life in
your years."
Abraham Lincoln-

The world is a drama in a dream

In between time and space
an incessant light
flashes to infinite.
Life and all materials fall
into the limelight of that
superbeam consciousness.
It is a labyrinth
and the cobweb of creation.
The mind of lives read
the matter, as it is tuned
to perceive the concept.

This world is an illusion
a dream colourful
and a nightmare too.

While in the awake state
the objects are

masses of feel

and felt by the touches.

When falling into a dream

the objects are seen

and felt

but does not exist,

it's a delusion.

In deep sleep

we disconnect

completely from

the dream and world

of awakening.

There is a watchman

when you are in deep slumber

who keeps the objects of

memory and all your

perception in his

custody and returns

your possession

intact when you

wake up and connect

to the body.

An ordinary life

is very much attached

to the materials

of world

and are attached to a body

that is the misnomer.

There is one

which is not affected

by the body consciousness

the seer of the

world

seer of the dream

the one who enjoys

the sleep and every

pleasure that is

available.

The body is just a vehicle

of the super mind

when your body

is no more workable

the supermind

disconnects

and moves in search
of another suitable
abode.

Great masters
like Jesus Christ
and Lord Krishna
had their mind
tuned
to get connected
and disconnected from
the world
as they wish.
There is only one
truth
God, the superpower
he sends a beacon of light

The world is a drama
in a dream

All in one
A flower blooms
in glowing exotic colour
with intricately designed petals.
The aroma spreads
a great feeling of freshness.

Moonlit night
star-studded sky
gracing puffy white clouds.
A star flies before your eyes
you make a wish.

At the serenity of dawn
the sun slowly rises.
His head off the eastern sea.
grains of mist drizzle
in golden granules
bluebird sings
in an enchanting voice
chirping birds
Your heart overflows
with joy.

Every object glows

with beauty and freshness.

Your soul dances with nature

become one with all.

Who enjoyed all the graces

of the lord?

It is the one

who is inside

the one who created this universe,

and he is the seer,

he is the enjoyer.

and enjoyment too.

All in one

the elated elevated one

who dances in ecstasy

of effulgence.

The dawn had arrived

Beyond the oceans
behind the horizon
night birds meet.

Kissing the moon
they bite the lips
of moon
exchange
a bit of golden glow.
The eyes of lovers shine
with the mystifying aurora
of belonging to each other.

The skyline changes
ambience
by drizzling moonlit.
Many stars and planets

rose and showered

astral lights of heaven

on lovers.

To watch the romantic

opera

flower queens

opened their eyes

slowly and sprayed

mist of fragrance.

In their merging

long embrace

they did not know

the dawn had arrived.

The glow of Adam's rib

At the dawn of my meditation

A mystic mystery was unfolding

Many a thought came and gone

My mind was murmuring incessantly

After sometimes serenity dawned,

a cascade of the golden mist of granules

A rain of grace from heaven followed.

I was floating weightless, without mind.

The entire world seems to be melting into

a brilliant ball of effulgence.

The rainbow, stars, moon, and planets,

were flowing down to the earth in colours stripes

along with heavenly-winged angels.

Suddenly a most beautiful woman

in her carved pulchritude appeared.

Her body was nude except for a creeping hooded snake.

The glows of Adam's rib were emanating off her blossoms.

While I was merging into the height of slumber,

with a giggle, she touched my body with her toe.

Stamped me with the elegance of her love.

She said wake up let us eat the forbidden fruit!

I am hungry enough to consume the world

Love me, Adam, and Love me again forever!

Moon dough Pizza

I found the chef holding

the moon

In dough shape

battered to silk.

He was turning and twisting

flashing, the smooth base

into the shape of the universe!

As an onlooker, I found his

swift hand turning

like a steering wheel
his other hand was honking.
Finally, the artist placed
the base into a full moon shape.
He was smiling.

The moon was decorated
with mushroom stars
glittering stardust.
He placed a comet
a piece of clouded cheese shredded.

I found many bits of planet toppings
It looked wonderful and yummy.
when he added a sprinkle of
mars dust,
Oh, it is ready.

Smartly he pushed it into the oven
a fine spicy smell floated in the air
my mouth was a sea of saliva.

Then with a smiley

he placed my pizza in front of me

what can I say

Artist chef,

Oh, you are wonderful, wonderful!

Cyanide capsule

Are we not planting every

step with fear?

The possibility of

a mine explosion

and your living body

turns into a red and white

a mess of a carcass.

Wherever there are

some crazy darkness

watching you

with an AK47.

Frustrated sleep escapes.

You turn and toss on your

bed of arrows.

Helplessly you cry silently.

Everyone runs for their life.

A load of your life

is dumped in a garbage can.

You curse your life

for the birth.

Nameless, powerless,

aimless, careless rulers,

gives you the promise

of a death kiss!

A cyanide capsule

Carbon Night

The entire city was asleep

discarding, tiredness of the day

dreaming of a fresh new day.

Suddenly an explosion

their dream vanishes into thin air.

People sleep walked

their food giver was a towering inferno

Thick smoke and fumes consumed

the air and city.

A wild cry in and outside the factory.

Union carbide factory was on fire

Many died on the spot

slowly poisonous gas-filled -air

seeped through the city

like giant strides

thrashing the buildings.

People who breathed

air succumbed slowly

into the corridor of the living dead.

Still the entire city

is waging a legal battle

for compensation

nothing seemed near,

except that the man

responsible was given

a clean chit by the rulers.

I drop a tear for

those disfigured faces of life

Making human patterns

Millions of years of history
were ground to each grain.
Time walked with each granule
filling the soul with sounds of nature.

We all came from different
sources of mass boulders
stretched through the length
and breadth into cycle metamorphosis.

Seasons danced with their
mighty steps dusting our souls
to a fine powder,
passed us through the hole of the hour
glass.

Wind tilted each of us
to arrange in a fine pattern

coloured with hue and mystery
of desert.
The aesthetic hands of 'The Great
the artist painted our life elegantly
framing on the golden easel
of dunes!

He is the one who decides
our fate
maybe many more millions of years
we live
in different patterns on earth,
until he decides otherwise.
to create another sand art
making human patterns!

My footprint

Always there is a shadow following me right from birth.

But I have to move ahead placing my footprint on the earth.

Believing in Rapture

She often haunted my thoughts
tickled my mind inviting attention.
I often ignored her merciless
pushing and pulling her visitation.

I found her beautiful, attractive
very sexy compounding her glamour.
She invaded my dreams daily.
Sometimes becoming a nightmare.

One day she pleaded to fondle me
to give her life in the wilderness.
She has slaved in the chain of time
clutched by fate boulders of cruelty.

So I decided to bring her out
I put her on an easel and sketched on her imagination
drawing her in black and white.
When finished I gave her a french kiss
Frenzied she laughed believing in Rapture!

For your next dawn

Celebrate every day as a birthday of your life

You are born each day from the arrival of dawn

Each day sun lights a candle in your heart

Moon blows it off making a wish for your next dawn

Dream Smile

As you stroll in the garden
there are beautiful flowers
with colour and fragrance
beckons you with the shower of mist.

Enthralled you view them with awe
invoking the grace of aesthetics,
dream walking through the
carpeted trimmed green lawn.
While resting on a bench
someone touches you with
Silky feelers of reed grass.
Out of nowhere, she comes

Sit near you with an exotic smile.
You imagine a flower bloom
in the courtyard of your mind
and wish to keep that flower
in your heart forever

The heartbeat of life

I am stretching

my legs for a while

In the solitude

of a dream lake

All the boats have gone

many travellers have

stepped on me

come and gone

Witnessed

many goodbyes

and happy hugs

I remain a silent

spectator

for the dawn and dusk

feeling the heartbeat

of life

5/7/5 | *Her ecstatic dream*

Her ecstatic dance

On silky lotus petals

unfolds a dew's dream

An elated euphoria

Just sit comfortably

Relax.

Close your eyes.

Breathe slowly.

You are on wings

of your imagination.

Floating.

Thousands of exotic

colourful butterflies

fly with you as guides.

This world fades out

disappeared far below.

You are on a flight of mercy

holding a hand of grace.

Slowly you reach into a

tunnel of celestial delight.

It drives you ecstatic.

Your mind is free from fear.

drifting in freedom.

Tranquillity converge

You laugh, cry and smile

with emotions unknown.

An elated euphoria

possess you with rapture.

You are on way to rhapsody,

reach in seventh heaven, Your paradise

dancing with love.

Pearls of words

In a sea of poetry

I just want to live

dive and swim,

roam and dance

as a tiny bubble,

just to float

feel the curving

waves

curl and cuddle

in my thoughts

that push me ahead

with the magic

of a metaphor.

Wings of images

carry me to

the fantasy land

of great poets
who live here
as icons of
freedom
forecasters
of time and future
who often used
to sound the whip of
caution.
The worshippers of
pulchritude.

Create magic
of words,
the drama of simile.

I want to live
as a poem
real and surreal
rhymed or unrhymed
free verse or just a scribble

Just let me be

In the heart of

love

to be pearls

of words.

A dream Maker

He came from obscurity, made a humble beginning

from the land of Mahatma.

A boy with high spirits sold tea at railway stations

while brewing a storm in the cup.

From poverty to spirituality, he moved with the steady steps
of a social soldier who trained himself to the discipline, walked
tall proudly as an Indian, and then a Hindu who loved all.

People did not like him standing on his legs

But destiny was written for him a magnificent role

The call of his state for his service.

Served as a volunteer for the nation

His enemies tried all black magic on him

They used voodoo charming to finish him off.

His image was tarnished miserably.

They all did their best in their quiver, but nothing could stop him

He marched ahead with strong strides.

They publically insulted him as"Tea boy" Urchin

Now he is the Prime Minister of India

Hope and aspirations of a billion and quarter of Indians

He is a dream maker for the people, a dream come true

I am sure the dream will come true soon!

Language of the soul

An expression of the soul is choreographed with fingers.

Thoughts and words filter through the fingers as symbols.

Eyestalk to a big audience effortlessly with movements of eyebrows.

All ten fingers express loudly in a language of the intellect.

Nine facial expressions visit the facial muscles for acting a scene

here the silence of fingers communicates with the heart's language

when the mind talks to the mind, mere signals will do the job.

Dream of delight

Solitude is meditating

In the lap of serenity

The Interior of the mind floats

as a lotus of divinity.

The entire beauty of nature

is manifested here

as the dream of the lord.

Awestruck I watch

the magnanimity

of the benediction.

From the silence

of mind, I delve into

the soul of tranquillity.

I do not wish to make

a ripple

a sound

a syllable

to wake you up from your

bliss.

In the vastness of

purity I want to take

dip subtly.

My soul reflects

In the mirror of your grace

You lie like a sheet of glass

visibly invisible

of your depth.

No, I will not disturb you

and wake you up

from the effulgence

I see my mind gets

crystal clear

by watching your

beauty and eternal silence

I just get elated

I leave you alone

as a dream of delight.

Prince of Fantasy Island

A magic wand in hand

turns you into a Barbie

adorn with the finest of

soft tissue gowns,

taken you in a palanquin

bedecked with

soft petals of jasmine.

You are showered

with chants of love

dine you in candlelight

with the prince of

Fantasy island

Serves you

with the rarest of cuisines.

You will dance

on a diamond

studded floor

with prince charming.

There in your bed chamber

a bed is made

with the finest of rose petals

you will don

in a nightgown

made of soft dreams.

You will be drenched

in an aromatic spray

emitting scents

of bliss

you will merge in a soul

of your dream

behind the veil of sleep

Lord's manifestation

Rhythmic Gayathri enchantments rise

as the dawn slowly lifts the snow veil.

The aromatic smoke of incense spread in the air

people take a holy dip in the sacred Ganges.

Sound, aroma and Vedic chants seep into nature.

Here life is an extension of nature.

Great saints heard and vision the sounds of Vedas.

Repeated what they had heard to the people

Thus the foundation of the culture and civilization was laid.

It is a pride that we preached to live and let live.

We practised what we had preached

considered the whole world as one community,

Every being on the earth is one family

The holistic family of the gracious lord.

I am proud that I am an Indian, who gave Gita to the world

a treatise for the day-to-day life, and secrets of death.

the creation, sustenance and destruction of the universe

I love to chat about my mantra in Sanskrit the language of
God

We are the ones who told the world the atom of life.

And everything begins from a circle, and cycles to a circle.

The inventors of zero confirm that there is nothing in this
world.

But, God, dreams of the Mighty Lord's manifestation!

Why I am a proud Indian because saints lived here.

Loving wait

Time just stampede

on everything.

Hoofing with force and power

with a stern horseshoe.

Yet earth bears the brunt

with strong silence

often she loosens herself

so the hoofs fall on wobbly

weaken the tap.

The purest of love

never fades

It will come back

with a strong

love tide.

When the moon shines

after a dead moon day

slowly he appears

on the western sky

as a piece of ivory

the hopes sprout

in the loneliness.

Day by day

the moon shines

bigger and bigger.

One day

he cascades

down into the

solitude.

Moonlit

your mind

you will be held

in a wild embrace!

You won him

with your patience.

Loving wait.

Cord of accord

My dream falls

into the depth

of wide eyes.

Long eyelashes

seduce my thoughts.

My words bite

the earlobes

Fondling the

cells of elegance.

I move ecstatic

shivering hands

chiselling

my fantasy into

dream.

Ultimately

striking a cord

of accord

Wonder tree

Once she was standing alone
in the loneliness of her remoteness
invoking nature to her bosom,
embracing time and tides.
Waves and winds of her emotions
subsided to her strength often.

Matured herself over the seasons
mind delved deep into the abyss
She realized her inner strength
became one with all elements of power,
put herself on an anvil of tests
burned in a billow of experience.

She grew into a giant
a magnanimous edifice.
Slowly every creature on earth

flocked under her shade of comfort.

Peace and tranquillity exhaled from her.

She turned into a resthouse of compassion

became a protective wall

for all the souls who found shelter in her.

She became their master and mother.

Mother of love incarnated.

Salute to the architect of wonder tree.

No Nonsense

Why do people talk of

what they have not seen

or experienced?

Vomiting all they

have grabbed

is an act of

violence,

it stinks.

One wise one

can lead you,

guide you to

cross the

river,

into immortality.

The stream

of life moves

because

both banks and

bed are

stratum.

never moves.

It is wise

not to talk

when

silence talks

sense...

No

nonsense.

Beacon of Love

A lump of coal

lives in a large mine

passed through

millions of years

climate stampeded

harshly

once a lively tree

consumed by time

blackened in the memory

lived as a Vantablack rock

turning into a mountain

of penance

the rock turns

into a diamond

Uncut but shines

behind the mud of

illusion

One dawn drains

the bowels of the earth

into a molten mass

of liquid fire

meditation of charcoal

continues

In the lava

time cools the charcoal

to the brilliant shine

a cut diamond

is born

with an eternal effulgence

time rests in him

as he has conquered

the darkness

to become the

beacon of love

Ecstatic tidal waves

She spread lying on the beach

wearing a birthday suit elegantly

intoxicated by the spirit of youth

covered herself with Goosebumps

Her blue-black hair gets washed

in the anxious waves from the sea.

the sun fondles the silky body softly

skin tanned by the warmth of his desires.

The body trembles every moment

as the hands of the breeze caress her

breasts of her passionate want.

Evening sun place his lips on her

She lies wildly and lazily relaxed

waiting for an adventure of lovemaking.

Her cheeks were pink with emotions
vermilion oh her forehead bloat.

Biting her lips she rolled over the sand
exposing her virginity with wild desires
making love with emotions she gets deflowered
by the manly hands of sunstrokes.

Gets disintegrated in the sweat of love
melts her virginity in the hands of strength
Exhausted and drained she takes a dip
with the sun in the ocean of unending desires
spreading, bloody vermilion of her womanhood
Up from the horizon, the moon drizzles a whistle
A star jumps in her mind in ecstatic tidal waves

A bouquet

I selected a few fragrant flowers

from the garden of my words

have only selective blossoms

in my garden of thoughts

I hope all of them are fragrant

from the scanty vocabulary

I have planted only plants of grace

But I nurture and feed them well

water them with imagination

Create a whole lot of sweet images

all put together and arranged in a bouquet

just for you with a wrap of imagery

and signed with an aromatic note

Cheer up lady even illness is an experience

Just smile away and be happy

make life a wholehearted grin

A philosophy of beam to an oddity

Deranged thoughts

Strolling in a dream

holding, hugging a big pillow

he lives rolling his eyes.

with fear, looks around.

life is like a fantasy

if he gets his share of a

piece of the psychedelic rainbow.

scared by a whistle afar

he tucks his head

in the pillow desperately.

a day without his joint

of smoke

is a day of the black sun.

he melts under the heat

waves of his brain

and remain

impotent like a sleeping

lotus.

remains stagnant

in the vein of a vibrant

crowds.

eyes dropped

acting Mister Droopy.

hanging his boots

on the forehead

he retires

until

a puff fills his

darkened lungs

and deranged thoughts.

A Thanksgiving song

There was nothing

but the thoughts of magnanimity

a format of aesthetics.

as he woke up from the deep slumber

of meditative bliss

he wished for the grand planet Earth.

It came off his body.

then the space for it.

he was in the total effulgence

designed time eternal.

it was existing in his mind

he released it.

From immaterial

the material arrived.

From darkness the

light emerged.

He listened to the sound

Space came into power

Then he dreamed land

deserts and dry lands

it became his part.

Sprout of plants

under the drizzle

He wanted life to
spread and grow.
The sun came out of his mind
then the moon and stars
to complete the
ornamentation.

He had oceanic dreams.
Life swam in the water.
Birds hovered over the sea.
Fishes became food for birds.
Giant monsters
ran over the planet Earth.

Then he engineered
the most beautiful
perfect intelligent creatures,
The man and woman.

He fell into a deep slumber
only to be awakened by
a melodious song

from the heart of man.

He is the only

creature

who praises the lord.

A thanksgiving melody of life!

Thank you, Lord, for resurrecting

In the hearts of humanity.

Fragrant air fills the soul

No, it was not easy

Shy and dry

love flooded

from our thoughts

soul and emotions

there was total

darkness

the moon was winking

flooding

twilight

I fumbled

while holding her

lips shivered

many attempts

at last

lips touched

lips lightly

her lips parted a bit

I sucked

her tongue and roseate

we bound our hands

each other

one tight hug

a tweaking sound

we made it

tulips

seeking

two lips

passion deluge

fragrant air

fills the soul

From the drizzle of blue lights

From the drizzle of blue lights

Winged ravens of darkness watched

millions and millions of

lives visited this planet

made their footprints

and impressions on civilization.

Moment by moment

the painter changed his

colour mix in the pallet

created a journey of sketching

the sceneries and raw portraits

of men who existed

by the law of survival

Life is a long journey

to perfection

many hands joined together

in creating the aesthetics

of scenes and scenarios

a perfect ambience was built

adoring with attributes of birth and death

in everything, there are unique fingerprints.

At the dawn of knowledge,

he saw the sun emerging from the darkness

enlightening the planets.

by the vision of wisdom

he created four Vedas.

Then preached the philosophy

of duality to reach

the one reality

the truth.

Life moved to the steps

of freedom

those who realized

flew away on the angelic wings

of freedom

overflying the crows

of ignorance.

The successful one

became the master

of delight and

brilliance by becoming

the king of wisdom

the ultimate truth

Honeydew

The evening sun-kissed lips

bloom

as a fresh rose

in the garden of my heart

with aromatic dew

I circle you

craving for

honeydew

Mighty ocean

Creating a mountain

of love around your heart

let me flow into your depth

as a crystalline stream

embrace mighty ocean

with a subtle fondle forever

Out of memory

The divine symphony

is grooved

in the disc of time

by his master's voice

the needle deciphers

the sound

by a rub and run for life

hidden voices

comes out of

memory

In the flame of my love

From the silent sighs

I hear you loud and clear

the firing desires of fantasy

each of my sinews aroused

as I see the enchanting curves

inviting me to hide in you

fondle your soft emotions

silky skins emitting the smell of nature

the musk of your lustful wild enthusiasm

a fire breaks out in me to consume you

the raw flesh of your tidal waves

enough to drown me in the moonlit

of your loving spasmodic convergence

I embrace your warmth

kissing the pearls hidden in the shells of

un-garnished oyster of your womanliness

let me present to you my body and soul

enwrapped in the flame of my LOVE

With her romantic dream

An exotic flower

opens her eyes to the east

receives

warm kisses from the sun

her dreamy misty

veil lifted

exposing her soft pinky lips

a thousand hues

pass through her eyes

fiddling the rainbow

she sprinkles the

aromatic colours around

The world gets

painted along

with her romantic dream

Smile of Muse
Somewhere from inside
Soft and subtle bubbles of a thought

muse fiddles with a silky melody
with the soul-searching

the mind finds meaningful words
from the lexicon of ancestors

pretending greatness
this poet concocts the words
thinking about a poem

the entire universe opens before the pen
like the bloom of exotic flowers

Outsourced

Most misunderstood man

once a breadwinner turned

infirm

looked down by

children and wife

as domestic help

free time free advice giver

no takers

but later realized

the value

spent force

living with a paltry sum of pension

takes a break with a puff

often retires

with a group of retirees

time teasers

who are forgotten

outsourced

out of the world

And your smile

From the infinite

train of time whistles

invoking memories

falling behind the morning mist

what a time that was!

we met and

travelled together

to the valley of our dreams

still, I can smell

soft fragrance

of flowering paddy fields

a ray of fresh sunlight

shining your diamond

nose ring

Even this night will fall

They squat

brooding over

a thought

how to

wade away

the night?

against the backdrop

of moonlit

they pecked

the darkness

on their pinions

soon to fly away

to the magnificent dawn

The first chirp

heard the first chirp of the season
she was sitting on the window sill
opening her beak for a clarion
slowly the mist changed into gold

the sun peeping from the eastern sky
a lively melodious chorus of birds
out of a dream, nature opens her eyes
remains a scatter of stars from the night sky

dawn theatre opens its show
fresh blooms of exotic flowers
they shake their petals rhythmic
the fine fragrance spreads in the air
a silky soft wind carries it inside
butterflies glide spreading colours

a drizzle of dew from heaven

pearl of a drop shines at the tip of a blade of grass

nose ring of nature glows a rainbow

life wakes up to a season of pulchritude

rhythmic belly dance of nature begins

I am the Atlas

A snapshot

I was carrying

the world on my shoulders

yesterday died forever

today this moment is mine

alive

tomorrow is yet to arrive

this poem is dead too

my words

are crawling creeping

off my pen

painfully I capture them

squeeze into

thoughts

imagination

are arranged on a canvas

painted

in quick strokes

as I saw them

with a vision

I put them

dipped it in colours

shades and light

embalm them with

the imagery

close my pen

with a metaphor

I am the Atlas

Who will cry for the world?

Dark clouds assemble around the world

who will weep for the world peace

no not you

but children and widows will

with the little hands and legs

they trek over dead bodies

In search of their lost daddies

battle fields of Syria and around the world

see the mass destruction in the war games

charred remains

burned houses

bombed city squares

skeletons

crumpled vehicles

scattered bodies

vultures hovering over

war games of

those stupid superpowers

chemicals they showered over the

beliefs and hopes of innocent babies

who arrive here generation after generations

with melted, crusted and decayed dwarfed bodies

pruned limbs

poor women lie stretched

In the pools of their blood oozed off

while modesty got raped by the cruel jokers

I shoot myself with pain

fire at the conscience of the nations of the world

come out of cosy petal beds

see the stark realities of the world around you

just say a word of prayer

listen to those painful shrill emotional sighs

don't you see weeping nature?

He is away from the clan

He is away from the clan

a dropout

rolling stone

in search of new pastures

different lands

experiences to learn

and live

facing the storms

and enemies

obstacles ahead

the journey began

when attacked by a tiger

always one has

to be alone to know

what is to be known

he came across

wild deserts

windy plains

wildness of forest

serenity of landscapes

murmur of wind

azure star-studded sky

as shamiana

an astounding sound of AUM

from the waves of the ocean

new lands new experiences

he is galloping with time

like free birds

widening the sky!

when will the journey end?

will he find what he is looking for?

fineness of truth

Bliss

All through time I was searching for my worth

embracing my toys

was sleeping hugged Teddy

dreaming of the sweetest possessions

In deep sleep discarded my dream

unaware of my body and senses

when I am awake I played with other types of gadgets

in the humdrum, I forgot to assess my value

went into a recluse there in the solitude

discarded all my toys, my attachments

In the freedom, I realised I am nothing

I know nothing I bowed down

to great masters to every being and non-beings

in the ecstasy of freedom, I learned my worth

It is smaller than the smallest and bigger than the biggest

larger than the largest, a heart full of saturated joy, my worth!

blissful blissfully blissful enchantments

The true colour

she had never seen her image

but had a dream about herself

it was a reflection in black and white

every cell of her body created

in a refraction

arrangements of tiny globules

chained in a string arched heaven to earth

once she got busted

smearing her colours all over the forest

had her reflection seen in a serene lake

Great one had painted and framed her

in a canvas of nature

now she saw her image in pure white swans

the base of all hues is pure truth

pigments just mirages

surreal pictures of the real nature

I had no idea

I had no idea
my fingers had magic
was fondling

a dormant hurricane
was sleeping
as a tiny seed

a clout
that can emote and grow
like a wildfire
my caressing wakes you up
from the folded hood
of lustful dreams
the ambrosia of love
flooded flowing
hot embers moan
cover
my face in the blossoms

Mimosa Pudica

I saw her glowing under the morning sun

standing erect in the full bloom of tender soft pink

her silky hair was shining in exquisite fashion

maybe she was visualising last night's rain

she was standing in her wide eyes invoking

the sweet ambience in the garden of life

with full of love and anxiety waiting for him

a sudden rip of hand she turned into Mimosa pudica

A tiny scribble

All through a cloud is hovering

the sun and moon are covered by

planetary positions unknown

gloomy doom pervades

high tides and low tides in the ocean

turbulence and choppy winds push hard

I row my boat alone since the childhood

pats on the back or encouragements were scanty

don't know why I was a dry leaf fluttering aimlessly

many stamped. stampeded

still, I do exist with my head high

with pride without prejudice

somewhere from the remote

an occasional vision of

bright light beaming at me

it lit my path with brilliance

could see the path clear

and clean footprints of my forefathers

confident, I trek alone

ignoring the staring red eyes

saw my dream flowers up in the sky

stretch my hands to pluck, it escaped to the depth of mystery

then an unknown hand hold my hands

my prayerful palms unfold

somebody poured the sacred water

oblation was accepted

in my palm, I saw a tiny lotus with shining dews

tiny scribble of my prayer on the petals

muse was dancing on it

What is not beauty?

from dawn to dusk a picturesque world unfolds with all
splendour and elegance, there is nothing ugly in this universe.
sun holds a torchlight flashing his beam sketches, Invokes
mother nature into the magic canvas, cosmic rhythmic music
passing through the holes of the divine flute. Clouds of
the western horizon change costumes each moment, The
humming of oceans, murmur of the breeze, dancing waves,
singing birds, their colourful quills, the beauty of ravens
their cracked voice', silky fresh sprouts on trees like hopes
for tomorrow. golden wings of flies, camouflaged lizards,
beautiful wild animals, Intricately designed cobwebs, insects,
a star-studded sky, and a lovely moon dancing among green
satin forests, and milky white ice-capped mountains. what is
not beautiful in God's creation?

To an oasis of love

The horror that shook them follows
robed in the shadow of sorrows
they trek a long way to unknown
the desert sun stooping close to their way
melting the sand

left behind all their possessions
carrying only their heads on their shoulders
they came a long way climbing dunes
still the debris of war litter the minds

lay ahead a sea of burning sand
storming the path
the hopes and aspirations plundered behind

targetted by the greed of Shylock
one fine morning they found themselves
begging for the mercy of death

the weeping women and children still echo

through the Valley of Devils

those escaped treks into fate unknown

chasing a mirage until the sun fades

when night arrives

they merge with the darkness

camouflaged

sleeping under moonlit

dreaming their villages

hoping for a new dawn

a new life in a new land

hopes always survive

shedding the dark cloak

maybe an embracing hand

guiding them to an Oasis of love

A deluge of the century

The sun absconding

thousands of bison let loose

stampeding

kicking the dark clouds

greyer clouds assemble

all over the sky

thundering

lightening

horizon is falling down

drunken intoxicated

pressure zones

mountainous oceanic waves

whirlpool

hurricane

sea waves churn the depth

rivers in spate

they gallop wildly

smashing the shores

frantic rain

flood

uproot trees

Earth is soaked, and the avalanche

landslides destroy

everything is on its way

thirty-three dam barrages

flush and rush water out

theatre of Hitchcock at the show

deluge in full swing

engulfing houses

farmlands,

bridges overflow

smashed

people escape

to the rooftop

their dreams afloat

Television sets,
computers
refrigerators
washing machines

everything in disarray
from huts to palaces

floating sun
in the sea, at last,
swimming back to the east
with vigour

I saw a peacock feather
floating
and a flute
picture Of Lord Krishna I draw
floats blissfully
oil painting intact
found his
meditative toe in his mouth
a smile on his lips

Attraction

beyond the veil of mist

In the depth of the pond

saw your half bloom lotus eyes

dancing in the blue waters

soft waves touching your dimples

your nose rings shine

as the sun sends his first golden ray

your image dancing with the dawn

a light breeze caresses your hair

earrings dangle with a chant

your flowing white silk Saree

caressing your rosy feet

where your anklets chime

horripilate sand grains

humming a celestial song

I saw you glide into my mind

soundless soft steps implanted

I carried you in a wave of respect

to worship as an idol of that love

you came to me in my dream

embracing the depth of imagination

The hiccups

The hiccups

long sputum blocked breath

chocked nostril whistles

for a bit of fresh air

oxygen cylinder is dry

blood pressure unsteady

round of faces around you

a sea of memory in waves

remembering the children

where are they?

Grandchildren, are they here?

Question reverberates

eyes closed tight

unable to lift the lids

the strong hand feels the pulse

feeble, the murmur

where is my wife?
History of memories flashback
romantic days
loving bodies!

Dreams unaccomplished
someone says not much time left
is it for me?
then I saw her
an angel with silver wings

don't know
what I know all this time
I served this body
cared and nurtured
fed well all these years to preserve
loving the body
have to leave now

No one loves you
except themselves
wife, children, grandchildren, friends
all love

loves their body

selfish

me too

once you realise

that the body is yours

but you are not body

the real love starts

universal love

is loving yourself

reflection of you in everyone

then you know

there is no beloved

except

you the self

the curtain falls

the blue sheet covers the face

weeping faces surround

symphony of sorrow

Her story

She started to toddle

with her little anklets on

jingling the valley with soft

rhythmic rhyme

little drops of pearl formed

into a silver stream

strings of a divine rivulet

joined her from the cloudy sky

opened her eyes with a dream

hanging in her blue eyes

under the arch of a rainbow

slowly she glided into the world

digging her path deep and clear

her journey started in the depths

cascading, jumping, swimming

through mountains, valleys and
hearts of plain lands

civilizations grew on her banks'
history of human life lies hidden
under her bosoms the ambrosia of love
many founded their living on the shore
humans animals birds all quenched
in her bed of magnanimity
fishes and others coloured their existence
she passed through a plateau
of life and death, extinct of species
all who approached her did not go empty-handed
bestowed her abundance
she still remembers her first drop of wish
from heaven
the end of rolling stones into a grain

gliding smoothly she sleeps
silently on the vastness of seamount
spreading her silvery hair of wisdom
and embraces the enlightened lap of her mother
and merge into the oneness of truth

Fool's Paradise

The idea and the ideal of communism just vanished

like a hypocrite's unconsciousness, just to sniff the smelling salt

time has changed, even before that the comrades were

a bunch of straight-jacketed buffoons are so idiotic

in the olden days of my childhood, I used to watch them

the communist small gods used to lead a procession

he will hold a red flag and raise his fisted hand in the air with vigour

with some silly illegible slogans, his followers will say "That is it"

without grasping or understanding the meaning of what he says

idiotic of them leaders were such when it was raining in Russia

they unfurl the umbrella in Indian streets cursing the bourgeoisie by adopting the stupid mannerisms of Lenin. Stalin or Khrushchev

they became leaders of Indian communism and pictured Cheguara

any ripple in East Europe to China in their internal politics

they argued forcefully about imperialism and expansionism

uneducated rogues roamed in the streets with red flags

stopped work and asked for wages as their right without doing anything

democracy helped them to gain power without any effort

when they came to power, the leaders send their children abroad

while the so-called comrades rotted in the filth of politics

all around the world, communism collapsed like a sand castle

what we see now is the vulgarity of communism as taskmasters

leaders and capitalists join together to rule billions with a red flag

poor subjects live in slum-like settlements with poor sanitation

Now we can see, Russian capitalism and Chinese capitalism
and pseudo comrades in India still live in a fool's paradise

I know this did not turn out well as required by the prompt
my words did not educate the reader well, I am sorry

My mother my master

Wandering through the world

wading in the tide of confusion

while dark clouds assemble around

and the black sun rises obstructing vision

there she comes the master my mother

she stretches her hands to hold

she guides you through the deluge

into a shore of safety and warmth

she teaches the real and unreal

infuses a hymn of truth. a mantra

between time and space the life

she takes you in a boat through

the flood to a shore of reality

teaches you to hold the oar

raise the mast when the wind is correct

then suddenly she disappears

swimming back to save her other child

her mission continues until then

she is my guru, my holy mother

Saint of eternity

Shedding the scaled skin

She started to climb up my spine

she was just a serpent

hiding behind my sleepy laziness

desires woke her up

treading slowly up the vertebrae

slow and steady steps

into the magic fantasy

she grabbed me

tickling my sinews to bliss

body was tweaking

powers of awakening energy

the further up and elevated state

the body became aware of inside moves

something was happening

blissful extravaganza

becoming aware of the strength

my queen moved ahead

all I wished become real

guiding me into the tunnel of brilliance

sounds and tone of words

turned sweeter

singing a song of awareness

my body escalated into a swing dance

my speech turned subtler

compassion flowed from me

I could embrace the world as it is

could not see any difference in it

lifeblood flowed incessantly

to create immortality

becoming a saint of tranquillity

I got intoxicated in the ambrosia of love

entwined with the mystery of eternity

Time changes

Time changes

moment to moment

the world transcends

we have no control

evolutions go on

Darvin's theory arrives at a stop

revolutions took place

the face of the universe changed

Man achieved a lot

from the genes of creativity

no fiddling with nature

turning space into a satellite junkyard

life easier

machines took over

the business of man

we became just numbers

analogue

alphanumeric

digital humans

bearing number plates

in our dreams and thoughts

there is a number

the day we are born

birthday

numbering continues

just imagine a life without a number

until ends up with a body bag number

in the confusion,

artificial intelligence takes over

every individual becomes a data

being measured

for a corporate intervention

each one is a potential

customer

to be tried and tested

in the deluge of

synthetic evolutions, the intellect of individuals

gets rusted

we turn into drunkards

nations of alcoholics

frustrated hippies

turning back towards society

we smoked weeds

marijuana

syringed drugs

Lsd

hollo souls

without any expressions

emotionless iron hearts

robotic legs and hands

pure iron balls

rolling

a life

children are born

by mere accidents

carefree

our souls are in corrosion

just need

an antibody

to clean ourselves

we had enough

antibiotics

now

let us loom for

an antidote

to clean out the mess

modern sphinx structures

like feelingless

robot-skeleton-human

a new anti-antibiotic

anti-robotic anti robotic

anti-artificial intelligence

system- that wipes out

all the data banks

then what will happen?

we will be humans again

with a sweet dream

hanging in the eyes

One day

An orchid collection

rare blooms in the garden

in every exotic colour and hue

hidden behind are

copy of species

birds, animals and insects

every life form is reflected

in each Characteristic

on the petal formations

awesome arrangements

of nature

in every human being

men and women

there lives a hidden animal

covering awful faces with a pack

protecting the fangs

hiding the teeth of the devil

to camouflage beast

beauty masks

shields to cover the real

wild instincts for blood thirst

one day

day of revelation

the monster comes out

breaking the cover

sleeping brute challenges

with a real thirst for blood

you are out on an exploration

destroying everything

bloodshot eyes staring at the world

Innocent smile

The bubble of time floats infinitely

each creature lives in its sway and swing

living in Pandora's box we glide and sail

into the vast ocean of existence unaware-

of the destination

like a stringless kite

hangs in the sky shaking and shivering

tumble down so deep into a whirlwind

outside a kicking and-picking world

so beautifully serene subtle and sanctified

the glory of each being complement

the entire universe rotates in a systemic path

each little creature adorns the fabric of space

the sun, moon and stars all being a part of the magic

out in space, there are angels and fairies

who came out crushing the ego of existence

they become seers of who lives in the present moment

smiling to us inviting us to break the hollowness

to join them in the magnanimous grace of freedom

wishing to break the egoistic, egocentric frame

and embrace the universe with the silky thread of
unconditional love

with an innocent smile of a baby

a smile that envelopes everything is spirituality

Smiling Grandmas

Early morning at the twilight

crest of the sun shows up

sickle moon goes down

grandma gets up

along with the trumpeting roosters

washed and brushed

with a neem stick, she is ready

putting sacred ashes on the forehead

saying a prayer to the baby sun'

she lights the sacred fire in the kitchen oven

tea kettle on the firewood furnace

off she goes to the cattle shed

cleaning, washing cattle and calf, milking the cow "ammine"
talking to her

In loving words and pet songs

then she takes her broom

sweeps the front yard

sprinkles a mixture of cow dung water

anti-infective traditional

Grandee runs to the kitchen with a sun hymn

prepares morning tea

filled in special 'golden brass' cups

carries to her sons, daughters, and grandchildren with

enchantments of divine names

by the time her loving family is ready

for a bath in the family pond

Granny supplies specially prepared herbal hair oil to each one

all family members wash swim and

hang to dry their clothes on a line attached to coconut trees

breakfast is ready

simple loosely cooked rice mixed with

green gram or whole gram

or just ground chilly, tamarind, onion salt paste for tastebuds

off they go for their daily work

some to the local offices, some to the

own paddy fields or coconut farm

Grandma happily sitting on the floor

for elaborate betel leaf chewing

extravaganza with tobacco and lime paste combination

relishes well after spiting the red saliva

In the brass spittoon

cools off a while with a handmade palm leaf fan

chants her prayers

while cooking the lunch

churns the curd with a wooden skimmer

butter is extracted swiftly

It is time now for a bath

goes to the pond her natural swimming pool for an oil bath

rushes back to the kitchen to arrange lunch

talks with her husband over a cup of black coffee and a betel
session

after lunch with all family members, goes for a well-deserved
siesta

evening coffee

by sunset lights an oil wick lamp

the fragrance of incense she reads loudly from the Ramayana

a chapter or two

dinner is served in the kitchen

mostly "kanji" loosely cooked rice

like porridge

early to bed with grandchildren

singing an old lullaby or folksong

or stories from epics for the benefit of children

She is no more now

but she handed over a tradition, culture and

civilization

her memory remains

an inspiration to the generations to come

it is not the gadgets,

we need smiling grandmas

Van Gogh

They are all born with golden hands

carried magic bristles

to encrust the face of the earth

had the brain filled

with sketches and scribbles of his hands

transcribing detailed pictures

each cell of Van-Gogh was filled with unique

colour schemes and frames

he looked into the world with an eye of a saint

mixed his thoughts with magic

painted with fervour

placed his bold signatures

the masterpiece was painted from his depth

it had the hue of freshness

and the colour of his vision

when he painted sunflowers

it was so perfect, shaming the sun

he had a slight peep into the depth of her elegance

and some flowers were shy

looking down

pale and faded, that was how the canvas lit

still the outstanding genesis

waits for the sun to arrive every night

for a wild embrace

sleeping on her chest Dawn arrives

Van Gogh holds his grin

Unaware dreamy eyes struck

Unaware dreamy eyes struck

rolled all over elegant curves

sensual imagination unclothed

saw your soft silky skin blush

vibing your Burgandy body

dimples turning red with petal kisses

Invoking wild desires slowly

erupting hidden heat waves

seismic convulsions

streaking into blushing lust

a dreamy bursting encounter

carrying you in a palanquin

paraded you in blushing nudity

entered into each other's silent depth

creating a whirlpool of prurience

releasing a tempest in the blue

we recreated our fantasy

consuming each other

embracing the body heat

sweat and smell of love

danced like ecstatic snakes

searching to eat the forbidden fruit

enjoying the fruit wholesome

were on a junket

exploring heavenly triangle

ejaculated lust

filling mouthfuls of pie

merged one another in magic blooms

Always

Always beauty created

diminishes every fresh gaze.

hear interior

jazz king

louder music

nurtures

originally preserved

quite reservoirs

sounding trinkets

ultimately venture

when Xylophones

yearning Zest

Works of art

Artisans create unique installations

intricate sensitive sensible works of art

exhibited all around the gallery of nature

sculptures and canvasses are on a display

great artisan of this world never sleeps

day and night he chisels out new designs

a great architect engineer at work

with a far foresight and intelligence

a strand of hair to toenails is an artefact

his build-ups last forever, as to generations to see,

beyond time and space

he arranged a biennale in the Garden of the World

Observe the green flesh of cactuses

in different shapes and styles

immaculately structured thorns and feelers

some flowers with exquisite flowers

desert bloom on the easel of imagination

every object of his manufactured

are beautiful and original

see his signature everywhere

realise the insignificance of man...

Somewhere in the Dense of the unknown

Somewhere in the Dense of unknown

grows a bush of creepers

the sun moon and stars rarely peep in

in the thickness of the forest, she was left alone

a seedling from the past generation

one day the rain arrived with fertility

rejuvenated her from the depth

waking up her from the deep sleep

yawning she rose to the reality

flint of sunlight energized her roots

sleeping buds active to the stimuli

sprout from the infinity

two little leaves and a flower bud

stretched her soft hands

trying to catch the sun

she turned into a sweet little girl

with beauty and elegance

at last a blue sunflower

spread her heavenly fragrance

the incarnation of the sun in the depth of the jungle

spreading warmth

many insects arrived

beetles and butterflies

Honeybees for her nectar

I dip and write this poem in the ambrosia of her love

Lullaby for the night

Fragile life tickle like a jellyfish

dimples blush on the cheeks of the ocean

the motion of unending waves lash on the shore

timeless sighs of sea chants primordial 'aum'

simple thoughts float in the mind

golden flints from the setting sun on my face

spirit rejuvenates from the dead dreams

leverage of time

sheltered in a cocoon

stumble words on a sea of rocks

a page filled with illegible scribbles

scar of deranged expressions

note my soliloquy in the wind

horizon is adorned with constellations

bottle floated in turbulence arrives with a message

the residue of imagination ticks in it

tapestry of images hanging on the horizon

corrosive dreams disfigure the paper

dark blankets cover the earth

tombs sing a lullaby for the night

The melted clocks drying out dangling on a cloth line

I walk through a dream, the melted clocks drying out dangling
on a cloth line

the persistent surreal world painted

topsy turvy in a magnificent canvas

the magician Salvador Dali created

his visionary world through the crystalline cubism

invoking the wonders of the world

in exotic colours, he sketched bold statements

viewed the world through the eye of a needle

sculptured the objects slim and more than life-size, unusually
tall elephants, giraffes

uniquely displayed crucifix and Last supper

premonition of civil war sketched soft-boiled beans

discovered subjects objectively and grew them into fantastic fantasy

titles reflected like couplets

wore a crystal glass and painted his themes

he had his springy moustache

well designed to suit his calibre

Dali Renaissance was created on the wheel of time

did I write anything about him?

Memories of scratched skin

With a lot of sneak outs

a lot of falls and skin scrape wounds

at last, I learned to pedal a bicycle

by placing my feet

through the triangle frame

oh what a wonderful

experience of freedom

only shortfall was

my inability to own a pedaller

for myself

all the money I saved

from scanty pocket money

was used to hire a cycle

one hour costing about

an 'anna' equivalent to ten, paise'

in my home, nobody encouraged

my cycling except for grandma

the day I learned

that I could place my legs

on both sides of the pedals was a victory day

proudly exhibited my skill

before my family including my father

although, the father was surprised by my adventure,

did not approve of my solo

ride to the village market

grew up pedalling into wonderlands

Grandma used my service

sent me on errands

when my legs grew

reached enough to sit on the seat and ride

I continued to explore

being alone I was in a magic trance

time travelling

under the moon and stars

floating in the blue sky lake

was flying with birds and butterflies

my boyish imaginations

once my elder cousin travelled

long distance to the next village in doubles

had to sit on the crossbar

near the handle

It was the day that pained my buttocks

showed me the star of pains

exploration to long-distance continued

made my college days

thrilling with my college mates

on hired cycles

we went on expeditions

to nearby earth dams

my desire to owning

a bicycle of my own

did not materialize

despite Grandma's recommendation

father did not like the idea

for fear of my meeting with

any accidents

film 'bicycle thieves'

added one more craving to own

my two-wheeler

but still, it remains

lifelike live memory

age of seventies my dream, my freedom

eludes when I am driving my own car

Holi in Heaven

From the galaxies

stream strings of colours

a laser show is opening

thousands of prisms refract

reflect

sending exotic images

inside a kaleidoscope

magician moon with a turban

magic show begins

the magician twists

his magic wand

the sky fills with patterns

clouds capture the multiple rays

spilling pigment of granules

Skyfall of rainbow

spreading tattooed wings

angels bungee jump into infinity

up and down the clouds

their exotic costumes

the veil on the face of clouds

kite festival

drizzle of stardust

canopy of clouds

decorated with stars

they belly dance with angels

sprinkling assorted shades of light

gods and demigods are playing

celestial holi in heaven

the festival of Colours

laser show

bouquet of lights

coloured fountain

dancing to the tunes

of cosmic rhythm

Rhythm of life

A special gem taking shape

dream of a mother and father

graceful boon from the great lord

he or she would be a Gemini an

exemplary planet in the solar system

ruled by the designer mercury

with wide tentacles of cosmic power

the infant in the womb of anxiety

is a celestial gift, a golden star

wrapped in a package of wonder

gracing under a ribbon of charisma

pure penance grooms, combs growth

of a pearl in the depth of oyster

Swathi star smiles

Gemini would win the world

with charming manners, etiquette
conversationalist who can lead
adaptability, outgoing, intelligent
sometimes very analytical,
at times impulsive as a trait

a diamond well-grounded
emitting sharp cosmic rays
attracting attention
will keep up the great traditions
pride of parents

moment of time awaits
to see the thrill of a mother's smile
happiness flooding
by the corner of my eyes
let the mystery of birth
reveal the secrets, Maya of life
may mother of all Mothers chant a hymn
rhythm and rhyme of life
pulsate blissfully

Flaming tongues

With thousands of flaming tongues

a little girl strolled into the valley kissing softly

her burning lips touch everyone on the way

putting her hot lip marks on and on

the charred faces exposed flesh

created a fearful stampeded view

donning a flame gown, she was on a devilish frantic dance

like tantrums of a little girl possessed

unable to bear the painful songs of nature

she flooded out of mother earth's womb

enough power in her lava blood to consume

this entire world of greed and selfishness

smiling and smoking she ate away the mountains

erected towering infernos in the cities

created dark creatures out of forests
Inflamed an entire continent like a cinder

took a dive into the oceans of the world
made a soft splashy giggle against waves
barbequed the sea fishes alive
walked with her thousand tentacles

oh, her loud laughter reverberates still in Pompeii
anklets sounding fearful everywhere
imagine if she drinks all the seawater
what if she consumes runs over the entire earth
with her smelting emotional lava
she was only looking for her mother

My muse sits on a lotus

Possessed by a foreign tongue

tongue-tied my journey started

scribbling my disarranged thoughts

carried a notebook under my arm

It was somewhat wet with sweat

one day my muse cried out loudly

desperate deluded, depressed

the stench of my emotionless words

on one fine occasion, she sneaked

exposed herself before a learned gathering

I was forced to read one of my ink spread

non-stop applause pushed me up

there was a critique of mine

who thought my scribbles

as schoolboy composition

he had joined the applause lately

I confessed my vocabulary so poor

yet, I write verses with feelings and emotions

my muse comes to me often

forces me to script my thoughts in

slanting, slanging, bending, kneeling letters

vocabulary turning very ordinary

my poetry is like a frog croaking

jumping, bumping like a flat stone splashed

on the surface of a pond

my frog resting on a lotus leaf

my muse sitting on a lotus winking

Like a Phoenix

Cosmic background score flows incessantly

the peculiar arrangement of notes and tones

a symphony orchestra is tuning ready

The conductor carrying the baton raises his hands

here streams rhythmic music

the bright curtain of dawn raises to the vision

with his golden crown and elegant attire

he jumps into the stallions-driven chariot

through the windows, he sends his cool rays

making the world get up from the hug of the night

peeps through every window and doors

announcing his arrival in the arena

old men and women rise from the bed

praying for a fruitful day on the stage of life

siren songs from factories the drama begins

play of greed in all walks of life

dreams hanging in the eyes of stakeholders

hissing, hooting shooting shouting

pandemonium mundane chaotically vibrant players

a spider weaves his wide web all over a corner

Spotlights turn in different colours and tones

background music streams for the scenes

many appear to disappear on the stage

grand charioteer controls the line

prompts the dialogue to each character

every kingdom, plant-animal, insect, flowers

comes to the full view of the limelight, pushes

remaining patches of darkness exposing the robbers

suddenly the director bungee jumps

along with his horses into the dark waters of time

to rise again like Phoenix with more light and fire

spider retreats rolling back the cobweb

our world fades in the darkness leaving silhouettes

Hidden art behind the lake of moss

A thick layer of green moss afloat

covers the dark waters of creation

painters squatting around the grand cosmic lake

fishing for golden-winged angels of artistry

all the great painters, sculptures, dreamed on the shores,
brushes in hand mixing paints in palettes while the master
painter sun

hide and seek in the oceanic waters of the sky creating unique
paintings, exemplary sketches of life and death

wading through the moss-ridden blue sky

they view his creations before he changes the display on the
horizon

all the Renaissance painters draw celestial inspiration from the
master

they found creating masterpieces out of the air

their images remain on the shore of aromatic rivulets of the art
world

Filippino Lippi, Scenes from the Life of St. Peter, Florence.
Leonardo da Vinci, The Last Supper, Milan. Michelangelo,
Creation of Adam, Vatican. Raphael, School of Athens,
Vatican. Michelangelo, David, Florence. Leonardo da
Vinci, Mona Lisa, Paris. Titian, Venus of Urbino, Florence.
Giorgione, The Tempest, Venice.

they made our world wonderfully beautiful

adorned roofs, walls ceilings Cezanne chapels

cathedrals of the world divine by their angelic

frescoes

Impressionistic painter, Frederic Bazille, in the trance-like
magic of the art world turned himself into a magician instead
of a doctor

impressions of inner eyes

made his

aesthetically bold strokes on the canvas

the special brushes on the pink dress

city walls and family reunions all give the best treat of the
master creator

they all sketched the dreams into the canvas

placing unique signatures in space and time

The mother of all mothers

The manliness of nature was in meditative sleep
was aloof and lonely Goddess Sekhmet
riding a lion she travelled through mountains,
valleys, meadows, grooves and streams

she was passing through a dream she created
mighty Maya, illusions and delusions
being the mother of all mothers she became
sum and sustenance
her every cell turned into a mystery of life
seasons arrived in her body,
sustained and perished

summer, autumn, winter, spring and rain
all wonders of nature flourished with her
entire galaxies, the milky way,
stars and planets, the sky, air, fire,

water and earth were part of her body,

rivers her blood, vessels, her navel

turned into the atmosphere, every cell of her,

Mother's magnanimity was part of this universe

with a thousand hands,

a thousand heads she became the mother of all

he was in yogic sleep her husband

were the liberator of life and the world

was crowded as there was no dissolution or death

manly nature was asleep

goddess-mother put her lotus feet

on the chest of the lord to wake him up

Godmother Sekhmet did a frantic dance

turning the entire universe into a dance floor

danced with her the creator, Brahma, the sustainer Vishnu

stars, planets, the moon, mountains, rivers,

oceans of the world, the forests danced along

when the lord woke up

to a dream of his Goddess

entire creations had vanished

behind the time screen

again to begin new sprouts of life

Author notes:

THIS IS A FREE TEXT FORMAT.

Goddess Sekhmet - Be Strong

Dear Goddess, please continue to bless and grant your blessings upon the love in my heart for my spouse and my child who is to come into the world in the last week of May 2020 and the love in their hearts for me. May no differences ever come in our path. May every obstacle in our path be crushed and every foe becomes a friend. May Charisma return home safe and sound post delivery with her baby close to her loving arms" in the comments box

Beam of hopes

When night attacks

day breaks into splinters

darkness envelopes

like the giant wings of time

a procession of thoughts

goes into the dark gully

intercessions are blocked

by the silhouette of fences

strong winds shake the steps

poor in the slums huddle

sharp piercing rain strikes them

blown out fuses of electricity

nobody to curse

they walk under the downpour

fully drenched into shadows
sipping country brew

with unsteady steps
dancing under the canopy of sky
they float in the wet shadows
looking at the ozone holes

they wade in the sea at night
hoping for a beam of light
to guide them into the dawn
their fresh hopes bloom

dark creatures from the valley
of thoughts stroll
in worldly images
seeking shelter from the storm
and rock cliffs ahead

The Mecca of cricket

Wide cricket ground in the southern hemisphere

the wild and wonderful island continent

where sports live in the lifeblood

nature is so graceful showering abundance

long stretches of plain land under cultivation

occasional bushes of man-made willow forests

enough, space, water and fresh air

friendly people grace with a broad smile

disciplined well mannered

the mecca of cricket Melbourne Cricket ground

welcomes by the statue of the

great fast bowler, Dennis Lilley

MCC exhibits the relics of master players

Don Bradman to Sachin Tendulkar

in a memorial wall hanging

all-time greats are weaved in

I was proud embossed faces

of Kapil Dev, Ravi Shastri

a long drive to Philips island

to see penguins and seals

fantastic drive on the great ocean road

and to see twelve apostles

found them shivering in the biting wind of the south

penguins had a tough time in the abrupt

the Sydney harbour with gleam and glamour

and the most photographed landmark

Sydney opera house

a wonderful creation in architecture

she floats ready to sail

take you off to the magic of opera

visit the rainforest by cable car

in to the heart of Aborigines

they dance in their colourful costume

often come back to memories

like a boomerang

set sail to see the great barrier reef

stretched to 2300 km long

View the culture of undersea coral reefs

an exquisite fashion parade of coralfishes

and marine life

at the plains of the cairn

memorable flight in the hot air balloon

seen the vast plains of Australia

she welcomes all with a hug of love

on our flight back

it was announced about the bushfires

after a few days

I saw her picture

was surrounded by ashes

like cinder

she was...

Sigh of relief

The days have come a long way
bubbling in a hot pot
long summer days burning
skin, boiling bloodstreams
Sweat pores filled with dirt
bacteria establish their hideout

in the soft petal face
they skated
skewing over the nose bridge
at last at the tip of the nose
a base, loom
a sudden sprout
filled with mystery

her soft fingers
caresses touch squeeze

fondle the sensual tips

a weak moan

worried application of...

all the creams available

mercilessly a squeeze

splashes out blood and pus

there remains a hill

red hot

painful, at last, a torrential rain

flooding

wipes out the cactus growth

smile of relief

Colourless colour

Against the backdrop of cobalt sky

where white puffy clouds graze

I saw her feathery wings satin blue

shades of her frame reflect

her colour was filtered in grains

angel was hopping from star to star

had her flaps grained of blue stars

she had the colour of divinity

dived she found dipping in the Milky Way

her hue had changed into milk

holding the tail of the comet she turned red

she passed through sunset

an exotic aromatic array of sprinkle

walking on the ramps she became a model

when I saw her

she was wearing colourless colour

the colour of her soul

5. *Simon Phelps Valley*

Roaring shouting

horizon

an assembly of hissing

hooting black bulls

ready to take off

for a wild-run migration

cowboys mounted

on their brown mahogany

stallions

sneezing

herdsman riding fast ahead

diverting the devils

whistling shouting kicking

the horse

rotating the lasso

to catch the running away beasts

threatening

lightning with piercing

glints

pounding thunder

stampede ends with

a cloudburst

carcasses of stars and

rainbow flood down the river

my thoughts rode past

the stretches of plain

to SimpsonPhelps on the valley

Expressionless face

Brick by brick we build cities

capitals, commercial centres

the industrial revolution made us look high

the sky is the limit

once we were living in dens

smelling horse dung

streets were strewn with dung

dark marks of animal urine on the road

the clang of horse carriages

sneeze of tired animal

track sounds of horseman

in the saloon lady

the gentleman

discussing silly anything

rickety coal-run trams

coal burning busses farting smoke

like in a magic
everything everyone changed
became fashionable
the city grew upward
skyline changed

the posh areas where hi FYI people lived
their limousines were parked under the building
moving palaces on the road
ridden by potbellied corporate
Madams and Pomeranians

nightlife
bar parlours
night clubs turned into
indecent exposure
nude dances
nude beaches
city belly dancers
busy Casanovas

the little pigeonholes

in the sky sway suspended

lit with laser beams

from the balconies

expressionless faces

displays the city by night

a psychedelic display of time

surrealistic canvass

changes the moods

of the city centres

Air-conditioned mind

A man comes to earth with an empty stomach

naked without a thread on

he was in the comfort of his mother's womb

lived about ten months among urine and excreta

was quite happy there in the warmth of love

then life continued

a journey to live and make me happy

plucked knocked acquired smashed

all the way ahead

ate, drunk made love

dreamed, acquired my dream

became big obese with filths of wealth,

obsessed with all fine things and thongs

yet I did not sleep, was very unhappy

strolled with a built-up of haystacks

became a Stone man

then one day I found a pig playing with

her babies in the filth

so happy they were

a beggar snoring deeply

smiling in his sleep

sound and happy sleep like a hippy on highs

happiness is conceptual

varies

I threw away all my Forbes grading

I air-conditioned my mind

Oh what a sound happy sleep I have now

Tweaking squirrels

The last couple of ripe mangoes also fallen
strong green leaves murmur in the breeze
sultry heat waves sweep through the village
airlifts hay dust swirling like a funnel

after a flourishing summer, the trees look empty
Summer rains brought little sprouts of hopes
tweaking squirrels bidding goodbye
the sun just dived deep into the coolness of the ocean

the aromatic cooking of the last supper of the season
Summer vacation is over
On June first the schools reopen
If the meteorological dept is correct
it will be raining tomorrow
tiny tots new to school on their first day

amongst opening ceremony

the newly admitted weep and smile

through the clouded Skyfall

all memories of many great summers

Visualizer

He finished drawing

infused powers of his spirit

he was on his legs

running, tap dancing

every day he visited his favourite places

sculpting images

filling, growing, reaching, teaching

he became a great visualizer

Under magnifying glass

Daily the sun wakes up

from the dead sea afloat

the eastern sea is lit with his glow

horizon is combed and swooped

litters of yesterday's heaped

dead stars, moon, asteroids

he gets up to a fresh dawn

her orange purple cheeks

first rays of his smile lit the earth

breeze opens the windows

singing a melody of dawn

joining singing birds and animals

The great gala opening of morning theatre

the soft fragrance of flowers

skipping butterflies in their designer attire

humming busy bees

the whole universe stoops

at your doorsteps

with a thud of the newspaper

our world wakes up from deep slumber

every word each letter

from the north, east, west, and south

speaks, louder

about, corruption, nepotism

rape, loot, arson

dumb headed politicians

their idiotic

while sipping the coffee

the scoops burn in your hand

consumed by the fire

like cotton the reader is

burned alive under a magnifying glass

Fashion statement

Moonlit lake, he floats leisurely
along with fallen stars of the night
underneath the surface, they glow
reflecting silver beams in the depth
like a laser display at a fashion show

vast lake sprawl like a sheet of glass ramp
breaking silence the symphony begins
frogs and crickets sing loudly in rhythm
the crystal ramp is lit with chandeliers

water lilies bloom opening their wide eyes
soft fragrance spread in the aromatic air
mermaids in soft steps catwalking on the rostrum
goldfish angels walk brusquely
fairies float on their designer wings

a sudden melody

she glides wearing a star-dusted robe

sparkles on her gown

her elegance dream walks

seducing the thoughts

sprinkle of diamonds around her

as she strolls moving her curves

A character

Nobody knows where he goes

regularly he boards a six o'clock bus

to the city

he was the only one in the village

wears a suit with a waistcoat and a tie

his shoes were polished and clean

often his netted faded red socks exhibited his dilapidated condition

he gets off downtown at the last stop

in the evening he walks down

with his faded antique umbrella now

a part of his torso in all seasons

With one hand in his coat pocket, he picks up peanuts

as if excavating it like a discovery

throws in his mouth with expertise and bites and chews each
one elaborately

on the dot of sunset, he sits on the same

abandoned beach bench

looking at the infinity listening to the hum of the ocean

he throws the remaining nuts to the assembly of seagulls

once again he looks at the purple waves

the spilt blood of the sun reaches the shore

he retreats with a deep sigh

Black roses of the metropolis

Some of the world's largest slums

they boast of created

where shanty dwelling holes built

with anything and everything

from plastic sheets to asbestos

mighty black holes

rats trafficking freely

stinking open drainage

dark liquids ooze twenty for hours

three sixty-five days all the lifetime

flows with the stinking liquid

the entire city is encircled

like a giant anaconda embracing

his fearfully wagging tongue

children take a plunge into the stone water

assorted faded jerseys of all the world cup teams

Pele to Messy and Maradona, Neimer to Ronaldo
cricketers from Australia to Sachin Tendulkar's number
famous number ten

the fog and smog lift the veil
feeble sunlight penetrates the slums too
children with a heavy backpack of used textbooks to schools
their eyes wide with hopes
of egg serving breakfast day

many smoke beedi and cheap
passing show cigarettes
policemen visit them to find all the theft properties
their boots stamp on the Holy land
Crushing the city deposits of filth and garbage

like maggot larvae
slum millionaires live
hoping to become future citizens
they grow up listening to stinky speeches
Of political eunuchs
black roses grow abundantly in the gutters of the metropolis

Oceanic poetry

I never thought that I would be a poet
It was Kevin who called me
I was sitting on the shore of the ocean
watching the magic of cobalt blue

veterans are swimming floating
scuba diving deep into
the depth of coral reef gardens
plucked the exotic flowers of poetry
in every colour, rhythm rhymes simile
there in the vast resorts dreamed with mermaids
danced with beautiful dolphins took rides

there they visited the Holy lands
Tranquil beds where the sun and moon rested, slept overnight
galaxies and constellations
black holes, Bermuda triangle
Shipwreck museums

they wrote about city-states submerged

extinct civilizations engulfed cities

Ploughed the floor,

cultivated seeds of new-wave poetry

exotic seaweeds

there is a Hall of Fame still active

where poetry is live humming in tunes

giant poets still live in the memories

all poetry is such s tranquil sea of action

our hopes alive in the pages whether I write a poem or junk
prose someone reads and posts a comment

Kevin reads every poem in his competition and puts his crisp
remarks

What a wonderful poet he is

so generous to write a comment encouraging the writer

I wonder if we all could meet one day

a poet's conference where we read our

creations

It might happen one day

Thank you, Kevin

our wonder boy of ALL Poetry.

A heritage-looking mirror

A heritage-looking mirror

adorn on my dressing table

the history of time hangs behind

darkened mercury coatings

a thin film of dust covers her face

daily I see my distorted image

an aloof and lonely image of mine

looks at me afar from infinity

she fades away from me

often she was far and near

Couldn't touch her face

evaded my hand feel

through the coat of dust

my face was unreal

then one day I found myself

wiping my reflection

oh, wonderful, the moon just
appeared showed face
lifting the cloud of mystery
confidence lofted my image

in the invisibility of crowded images
I walked dreaming
was thrilled and filled with metaphors
you were so near
yet afar
divided by a screen of clouds
now we met
seeing seeking being
in the reflection of a ripple less lake
in the depth of serene love
behind the fogged mirror
real self was hiding
with compassion, love
filled with happiness ecstasy
just one wipe by grace
a beam of light
started emitting from the
infinite darkness

Dancing floor

Nature is dancing

her ecstatic frantic spin

on the entire universe as a stage

decorative stars

confetti of celestial beads

spiralling meteorites

drumming comets

Glittering stardusts

constellations

flaming planets

moonlit skyways

cosmic stage settings

there are daisies

as cheerleaders

their pom-pom displays

each girl smiles emitting
Green, blue purple and red
beams on the dancer's face
spotlighting
rainbow schemes on the spot

what a cheerful
grand galactic gala to watch
a vast stage show
musical extravaganza
nine dramatic facial expressions
lime lighted by the flowers

the entire cosmic show
unfolds before the world
with pomp and prestige
from atoms to galaxies
takes a spin in the ballroom
merging with the mood
of time

Night sky

Night sky
a blue designer sari
spread far and wide galaxy
the twinkle of gems, diamonds
lavish brocade made of
Diamond, Ruby, Emerald,
Yellow Sapphire, Garnet
Blue Sapphire, Pearl,
Cat's Eye and Coral.
constellations on borders
horizon littered with stars

flashes of thunderbolts
it's roots Pierce dark clouds
cascading wings of angels
far away drizzle of fireflies
sparklers In a Night show
moon swings in a bungee string

comets ride a stallion

in a swan-shaped

chariot of colourful clouds

night queen rides

her nose ring shines, anklets chime

sharp penetrating ray of elegance

my eyes reach into

a whirlpool of azure space

floating in an ecstatic dream

flying to the eternity of time

Songs of the Soul

At the auspicious dawn hours

she wakes up from the depth of deep slumber

stands still with her silk nightgown on

watches the golden boy rises from the eastern ocean

his long blond hair wet dripping colours

sitting cross-legged she sings a melody of oceanic music

repeating seven classical notes in different tones and styles of
Carnatic music, praising the lord

her silvery anklets tapping rapping

on the beach

the wind carries the rapture far and wide

after dawn when the sun reaches the height of ten- o-clock the
sea music turns to Western classics

blue waves move like piano keys

vocal melodious tones of heavenly notes

till dawn to dusk the oceanic waves

dance on rhythmic cobalt waves

surging and surfing excited

on the blue water opera hall, the musicians performed

Ludwig van Beethoven

Johann Sebastian Bach

Wolfgang Amadeus Mozart

Johannes Brahms

Richard Wagner

Claude Debussy

Intoxicated waves conducted the orchestra

while Eastern music masters

performed classical Hindustani and Carnatic concert's on the
blue rostrum, Swami Haridas, Tansen

Ravi Shankar, Bhim Singh Joshi,

Ustad bismilla Khan Allah Rakha

Carnatic masters Thyagaraja bhagavathr, l

Lata Mangeshkar

Mohammed Rafi,

the entire musicians of the past

present and future does daily episodes of music flotilla

turning themselves into ocean songs

Seven seas are seven notes

exploring seventy-two moods of celestial musical streams

the world is divided into seven platforms conducting musical
nights

I scribbled some words dedicated

to great creators and conductors

of divine songs of the soul

First smile

On this day baby, you lit
a special smile on Mom's lips
created heaven around us.
Daddy took you in his hands like
pink lotus fresh bloom from the
lake of his Manasa Sarovar

our life became so engaged
caressing you comforting
precious lively moments
the first godly smile that bloomed on your lips
aroma, your milky fragrance
pinkish soft gums beam

thirst, hunger all noticed
by your gestures and fed you with
my milk of compassion

watched your hands move round

legs cycling thrilled

and your first voice to call me mom

your first turn on your belly

let me bake a cake of my love

decorated with sweet creams

of my hopes, the first candle on your

birthday cake

a wick of my gratitude to the lord

kiss for you a special motherly kiss that you will remember

ever

because it is filled with dreams

hopes and blessings for your journey ahead in life

Rhythm ecstatic

Cerulean depth of intelligence

cobalt waves weave a satin robe

the silver lining brocade at the shore

where stars twinkle on the beach

the rarity of her deep blue eyes eternally youthful

calm and peaceful ripple less mind

body heaves in rhythms of ecstatic sighs

she houses a plethora of surprises

a brave new world of marine life

behind turbulence, their lives

a tsunami of emotions, the tempest of hunger

hurricanes of chivalry

typhoons of challenges, yet she remains composed

coral reef gardens

incessant chant of a primordial mono syllable AUM..........

A character

Nobody knows where he goes

regularly he boards the six o'clock bus

to the city

he was the only one in the village

wearing a suit with a waistcoat and a tie

his shoes were polished and clean

often his netted red socks

he gets off downtown at the last stop

in the evening he walks down

with his faded antique umbrella now

a part of his torso in all seasons

With one hand in his coat pocket, he pulls out a peanut

as if excavating it like a discovery

throws in his mouth bites and chews each one elaborately

at sunset, he sits on the same

abandoned beach bench

looking at the infinity listening to the hum of the ocean

he throws the remaining nuts to the assembly of seagulls

once again he looks at the purple waves

the spilt blood of the sun reaches the shore

he retreats with a deep sigh

Portrait of a Tailor

Portrait of a dark photogenic man

very sharp shot in black and white

efficient usage of a photographic plate

skilfully washed in a dark room

like apothecary in the village

he occupied a coveted position

the busy only tailor in the village

was leaning on the machine with his thin round framed
spectacles on

hand-operated vintage singer machine

used to produce the sounds of a generator

he was the favourite of ladies,

an expert in women's clothes

a lean man one-man industry

to collect and deliver stitched materials

I have never seen him wearing a shirt

half-folded lungi fastened with a wide buckled green canvas
belt

added with two pouches at the front for stacking money

walking in a rhythm moving his back

synchronised with his lean legs

hair cropped close to the scalp

decorated with silver strands

bushy eyebrows

raising vellus hair

a half-smoked beedi on his ear

his chest was covered with grey hair

I saw his picture on the last page of

family album with a medallion

must have used his picture for a photography competition

in the portrait category

Silky muslin

Pure silk muslin
artistic curves
Pearl Dew web robe
glide on marble

moonlit aura
breath of breeze lifts
her gown upwards
a lily bloom

At the bottom of my life

I had about 1000 books

when old age crept into my skin and bones

loosened my sinews

dust and worms attacked my books

my looks

distanced me from the bookshelf

Charles Dickens, William Shakespeare

Dante, Emile Zola, EM Foster, Pearl S Buck

Victor Hugo, Sholokhov, Maxim Gorky

Kalidas, Vyasan, MT Vasudevan Nair

Basheer, Uroob, O V Vijayan and many more

Started shouting from the pages

There is no way to caress the console

the geniuses

step ladder had been removed

to save me from a bone fracture

brought them in from second-hand shops.

Had bought from the heaps at the railway stations

read them on my shuttles

back and forth from office to home in Mumbai

they were my great teachers

balanced the thoughts, opened doors of philosophy,
spirituality, literature

dramatic process, drama, poetry

When I published a huge collection

of my poems and entered my little name in the Book of
Records

I put a small signature at the bottom

Of my life

Ballet show

The. Morning breeze wandering
spreading the fragrance of the fall
the cottage still blanketed in deep slumber
grazing snow clouds move down

sprinkle of dew on the meadow
tickles the feet with a heavenly fragrance
Pale sunlight sprays golden mist
thrilling assortment of fresh blooms nod

like a shadow show images appear
natural ballet dance in progress
emotions step rhythmic with artists
great showman spotlights the drama

Songs from heaven

Once he used to trumpet and gobble

proudly head high beaming

inviting his sweet hen

the lady met him with her best attire

black and white feathered quilled robes

exquisitely dressed

when Easter and Christmas arrived

hid behind her lover

with hopes of protection.

despite, destiny driving her into

the cage of uncertainty

was sold out to a butcher

soon was processed

mechanised guillotine chopped the head off

laid to rest among other million heads

her beautiful crown lies in the dustbin

she was bought by a rich man

dressed, baked, rolled in delicacies

turned out to be a beauty

ornated, miss world

attending turkey dinner

dancing, drinking cocktails

miss world was consumed bit by bit

her body was dissected

into pieces

at last she,

her body vanished

skeleton cast away

unceremoniously into the garbage can

I can hear her singing from heaven

"Mary's boy child Jesus Christ was born on Christmas day"

Say sorry general!

bullets were fired from the guns of gen. dyer.

unarmed villagers were caged by the rowlath act

scream of fear leads them to jump into a well

thousands of women and children

chaos, confusion cruelty of British slave masters

created one of the devilish acts in jawalianwala bagh.

still, the ground is littered with red flowers

General still, dances with his sword of honour. Say sorry devil.
It is time

A dew in my heart

Suddenly her head rises

from the pond

thick black hair beaded

with silver globules

glowing in the golden beams

she was floating

pinkish silk body

covered in a thin sheet of

cascading water

wet cloth covered her bosom

slowly she toddled up to the steps

the foam of toilet soap

covers her velvet skin

an aroma spreads

I was taking a morning dip
in our village pond, it was like an open bath place
Young and old take their bath together
shyness was not covered by their freedom

a side glance met between us
with a shy smile, she retreated

I still remember
the lotus bloom
pink shaded petals
morning dew on her lips
bees, butterflies and beetles
visited her, tasted her honey
roled in pollen

humming a romantic song
my legs took my way
she stuck like a dew in my dreams

Lost dreams

It was a long walk to the pond

crossing an infinitely spread paddy fields

trekking through the ridges bordered

yellow bloomed little tree plants

song of cricket and grasshoppers

leaping frogs with a protest

bare footfall the ice-cold dew on grass blades

a sort of fine feeling rises all over the body

while the cool breeze feels goosebumps

humming a popular old Tamil song

legs lead to the pond where entire villagers take their morning bath

the water is almost green with floating moss

there was a long wooden plank fixed to the shore

a strong platform for divers

straightforward we run over and dive

a splash of water that irritated lady bathers

now the pond is no more

instead, there is a housing colony

sprawling with tall buildings

Paddy fields have vanished into shopping malls

melody of insects lost in the blaring horns

where is it I am searching in the lost dreams

Fantasy land

It was a guided tour through Hobbiton

a fantasy unfolded before the eyes

each grain, blade of grass

bonsai trees dwarfed land

of Lilliputians like extinct race

once, sturdy men and women lived

in the magnificent land

true to life exhibits at the fairyland

found life was infolding

their possessions

small fields, miniature trees

animals grazing in the meadow

little streams trickle down

tiny ploughs, grinding stones

round tables with onyx chairs

granite paved roads
Lilliputian huts
all came alive from the memory lanes
history was unfolding

women and children in their
colourful costumes
the spray of ancient perfumes in the air
sounds of a unique dialect

we old men with backpacks
toddle and a Chatterbox butterfly

suddenly the announcement
wakes me
The tour ends tomorrow.
Where am I?
thermal steam comes out
Of Hobbiton settings
riding a lama while Kievs lean slowly
rhythmic music of
Maori people

The blissful life

Mother of all mothers

the lioness of forest

incarnated in her most benevolent form

transformed into a classy lassie

laced in an oceanic blue

wavelets cascading

vine creepings decorated with exotic blooms

silky flowers nodding

dancing to the music of the breeze

aromatic nature

exposed her exciting body cultures

a half-dreaming smile

in the corner of her lips

while her darlings play

tickling her gorgeous form

while the lioness waiting

for him

her macho man

king lion of the seven continents

her entire body craves

singing a romantic melody

blissful life

Revenge by starvation

once he was booted out of a British train compartment

his fallen teeth, humiliation to a young barrister

there fell the crown of the British empire in the dustbin

that young lawyer invented the struggle of starvation

of a non-cooperation, bloodless revolution

he discarded the fashion statements

wore loincloth

made Winston Churchill sit before the half-nakedness of
an Indian saint to declare, and sign a treaty about India's
independence. end of a sweet revenge

A woman of substance

Every moment she changes her attire

some times frilled brocaded saree

an exclusive edition oceanic satin blue gown

intricately embroidered with silvery strings

she is a cat walker in a fashion show

spotlighted under the multicoloured

LED sunbeams

dressed in trendy attire she rolls over the ramp

exhibiting elegantly designed outfits

times sober soft subtly sexy

strolls over the beach shining smiling

rough and tough at the time of mood change

a romantic, fashionable strong woman

commands the entire region

She was my dawn dream

Luxurious dawn arrives
slowly from the silence
the magnanimous backdrop
filled with cool blue granules

from the blanket of deep slumber
morn still snores for a last-minute sleep
head tugged in the foggy sleeping bag
cuddled hands together in a coma

my legs stretched for a morning walk
early birds pecking at the beach
chanting pigeons with louder hymns
I saw her parting the screen

her long artistic fingers wade in the mist
she was in an off-white nightgown

petal feet floating in the air

angelic wings move like windmill fan

her eyes wide open watching the world

my pen sketched her like a selfie picture

my thoughts filled with her image

I scribbled her beauty with indescribable words. She was my
dawn dream.

Reminiscence

Many butterflies hibernated
in the brain cells
passed out with flying colours
from the fashion schools

like celebrated models they fluttered
their designer wings
exhibited on the stigma ramps of
fashion shows

exhibition centres around the world
from flowers to flowers they flew
carrying their body slim
In a jewellery case
the fantasy of the outer world

under the floodlit ramps

flashes of the photo shoot

she lived in dreams

fashion pages

savvy magazines

the short span of a butterfly's life

age licks away textures

they retire in an obscured corner

pigmented wings

adore the hairdo, s

reminiscent of the angelic vision

walk around the street

as fitness freaks

Red hot lips

Red hot lips

mascara beams

sky shaded eyes

the first night she smeared

paints on him

Storyline

The overcrowded metro train

people squeezed in like sardines

early morning suburban train

white collar and blue overalls

the eyes are drooping with hangovers

lids thick with sleeplessness

Lucky ones occupy the seats

habitual rummy players

women their faces fixed on books

turn the pages in rhythm

fellow passengers busy reading their favourite columns

gossip pages

executives skimming through reports

all the books I read were second-hand books

bought at the entry points of the station

then sold off at the other end after reading

magic mountain passed through

Emile Zola's Nana was dancing on the platforms

am I in 100 years of solitude in the sultry compartment

Gabriel Marcus smiles

Atlas just shrugged along when the electric train jolted

Ayn Rand sits in one of the stations

a mind filled with words picked from the

streets

there is a storyline

In every breath

[Sprouts of her spring dreams]

Sprouts of her spring dreams

bloom of sweet fragrant flowers

she became parrot

Season parade

she was a sweet pink girl

with a little ponytail shaking rhythmic

fresh fragrant petal cheeks

roseate lips of vibrant spring

season dressed her up

exquisite elegant exclusively attired

a young lady adores the ramps

the drizzle of pulchritude

now the hot spotlight shines

Summer sun over the head

heat waves, perspiration dry earth

my lady arrives in a bikini

scenes and ambience change
she wears a bold leather jacket
her mink coattails
blueish white snowflakes flutter

fall comes like a shower of confetti
the murmur of coloured dry leaves
then shower a welcome drizzle Of monsoon

[Magic show begins]

Magic show begins

grandeur of galaxies

tulips hypnotized

Star-lit night's halo of the moon

Yakshi the Fairy Queen

intoxicated sits on her back

standing trajectory wide spread legs

Invoking splendorous entire creation

every living and non-living manifest

each bird and animal nested in her bosom

her eyes open to the seasons

captures the blissful identity

star-lit nights halo of the moon

colourful passerines golden falcons

rainbow winged birds retreating from college

giggle and louder singing

seasons reflect on her countenance

fresh Sprouts, exotic blooms

Autumn falls of assorted colours

dreaming rainbow, summer rains rounded hails

whistling winter on her nostrils

new angelic winged visitors from heaven

she sings a song for every season

Ripple less placid lake

ripple less placid lake

a breeze tries a light breath

circle of waves glide to the shore

splinters of blue glass splash

in protest a frog leaps

blue satin silk swing with

the face of the moon dissolved in the water

distorted image

azure sky spills indigo into the lake

water lilies awakened

they were in deep meditation

splash of a silverfish

silence again

The tent she pitched

The tent she pitched

camouflaged with cascading sky

rooftop adorned with candelabrum

crystal beads glass vases

coloured decorative constellations

lively dancing planets

divine cosmic music

piping down to the tent

tongues of campfire lit her elegant face

the smell of nightfall

songs of night birds

tree of fireflies

artisans draw magic patterns on the obsidian tablets

legs up eyes fixed she glides

through words

sickle moon peeps through

a golden cloud emerged

remembered her lover and his naughtiness

she dozed off for a while

realized she was a little star

playing with faeries

becoming a speck of celestial dust on the vast canvas

lost track of

the time date day and year

Bluebird pen

A mountain of darkness

night seeps slowly into the world

obsidian, ebony wood and carbonado.

screens of nightfall

fearful creatures

croaking ravens announced the

the arrival of the dawn

through the creek of the mountain

the shine of pure morning

mixed with white snowflakes

fluttering glittering

hails of last night are still, rolling

azure sky

littered with grazing white puffy clouds

nodding tree branches

golden needles of the sun

pierce through leaves

songs of Nightingale

does it have a colour

yes the colour of love

my black ink

white paper

bluebird pen

Dream unfolds

The astrophysicists' ornithologists

astronomers with their heads up

peeping through the binoculars and telescopes

the huddled azure sky littered with

constellations, galaxies

Blue diamonds twinkle

sending waves of lightyears

Milkyway is glowing flowing to eternity

indigo coloured Whirpool

angels display

elegant designer sapphire wings

sky falls in blue snowflakes

cobalt winged fairies

adorn the trees as winter blooms

queen butterflies dance ecstatically

cerulean satin clouds

assembled in background

for a celestial show

the show begins with a blast of confetti

sparklers

dream unfolds

Aloofness

In the frost of the night

she awaits for him

detached aloofness

melancholic spill

silhouetted dark light

even the last Nightfly retired

End of a wedding

The hall was littered with

crushed faded foul smelling flowers

a lone brass wick lamp flame weeps

raising smoke

plastic chairs in disarray

some of the fans still rotating

ashtrays full of cigarette butts

emitting filthy smell

betel leaves areca nuts

scattered on a tray

caterers enjoying the leftover dishes

several scoops of ice cream

an old romantic song

repeated in the speakers

one by one the lights off

the tail of a decorated limousine
just passed through the exit gate

stray dogs had a feast full day

they are busy barking at each other

for no reason

A thick fall of black mist

A thick fall of black mist

wild ferns' strong prop roots

entwined vines on giant trees

the forest hugs the lonely night

glowing stern eyes of owls

burning charcoal hot eyeballs of tigers

cheetahs, wild cats

the incessant chorus of forest

the symphony of Jungle

in the sleek openings

a shower of moonlit

twinkling snowflakes cascade

moon swimming in the lake

along with mermaids

a lone bull elephant takes a shower

his trumpeting breaks the four corners

night flies, bats out searching for food

in every corner hides a mystery

Missile Man

Many come to this planet,
Live dead and return dead.
Some live and depart silently.
Most lives to eat and die.

There are some who walk ahead,
With a dream in vision.
They are the ones who lived,
Placing a footprint on the soil.

In an obscure fishing village,
At the southwestern tip of India,
There lived a boy with wide dreamy eyes,
He had hidden a dream in there.

Riding a bicycle he stretched his hands,
Reaching for a rocket to infinite.
One day he made up for it,

Flying on the wings of fire.

He strode ahead of time leading the world,

Placed his signature as road marks.

Dr.A.P.J. Abdul Kalam lived here,

With a wise twinkle in his thoughts.

He ploughed deep into minds,

Planting seeds for the future.

For children, he erected flowery arches,

Sitting with them underneath,

He coloured their dreams.

invoked and initiated them to a brave new world.

Our president is a simple man, a saint,

With a simple life became the people's president.

He took very little from the earth,

But returned everything in full.

Even the love and respect we gave were returned to us in full

Left us with an open hand and an open smile

A simple and easy abode to heaven

With a smile.

A humble salute sir.

Silky thread

When you enter,

my face blooms.

I cuddle you

in my dream.

Bind you

with a silky

thread

of love.

Silhouette

He had a collection of pictures.

A gallery of beauties and butterflies,

They came into his life,

From different walks of life.

He met them regularly,

Becoming beauty and the beast.

His life was silhouetted.

He marched through the arches,

Holding her hand.

Flower petals showered on their way.

One day he found her lying,

Among skeletons from his cupboard.

To fish

The mind squats

with a hook and line

to fish thoughts

Sculpture

Invoking the subtle soft image of his dream

he sculptured an angel from his heart.

his chisel and hammer deciphered

a hidden beauty behind the harshness

of hard rock.

Like an archaeologist, he brushed out

the grains hiding in his imagination.

Meticulously he kissed each granule,

gave life to the hidden idol of his vision.

every curve and dome of excellence

was given existence in his celestial imagery.

then he took a deep breath and infused

his lifeblood in the veins of his Diana.

She glided away into infinity holding his hands.

His body was found floating in intoxication.

He had his hands severed why?

Freedom

Crack the shells

liberate yourselves

To the dawn of

Freedom

It Was a Serene Land

It was a serene land

Quiet and peaceful

The sky, the sun, the moon, the stars-

all gracing in abundance.

This land was tranquil

Always bathing in a celestial downpour

When the rains come it drenched itself in purity

Filling the earth with riches

Then new seedlings sprout

The mountains kiss the sky-

blushing its face in the rainbow.

Melting the snow and flooding

The valley with milky-way

Towing the clouds from heaven

Peace and silence play hide and seek here

All the creations begin here

Creatures big and small live nearby

The fresh silky leaves from vegetation
Flutter and dance in ecstasy
They kept this land sacred
Their forefathers sleep here
Their culture, their hard toil
The enrichment with divine intuitions
It's a land ruled by the chieftains
Who had their self-righteousness to
Sceptre. They ruled and lived
For the laws of nature.
They had their nobility as crown
Feathers of manliness

Until one day

There was a shrill cry from their children
Then a sigh of their women
The land had been invaded
The wild horses who were the
Roaming spirits of the land
Was running helter-skelter
Their tails are up and flow
The wild cattle were

Stampeding their land

Everything disappears fast

Their sacred burial places

Were run over.

Nothing was left

Their women raped

They left nothing untouched

Evil hands fouled everything

They came in trains

Carrying guns and gunpowder

Chewing tobacco and smoking

They invaded the privacy

Spoiled the poem of the land

Dig deep for gold

Ploughed the soul

Planted the seeds of greed

And plundered the virginity

One day every sand on that land was

Drenched in blood

The Yankees, the mercenaries

The desperados, the fugitives

The thieves and robbers

All plundered the good earth

The chieftains fought and

Went in retreat

In to a loud silence

The Whiteman's burden was

Lashings its whip

The entire land was run over

Hoofing on the dunes of

Lawlessness

There was no mercy

The children forget to cry

The deep sigh of women exhausted before it started.

Time galloped fast

They erected monuments on graveyards

The wisdom of chieftains buried

Under the tomb

The settlements came

On the fallen dreams of natives.

They erected their skyscrapers, trade houses

and world Trade centres

With the bones of Red Indian

They erected showpieces depicting the greed

One finishes the job

They looked all around the world

Making dollar signs everywhere on the booty they found

Made the world a miserable place to live.

Oh lord they don't know what they are doing

Forgive them. Forgive them

Chime chime chime

I heard a ding dong

waking me up

then a TungTung

from temple tower

dong gong gong

church bell

train turn turn

cycle bell of the milkman

HongHing hond

paperboy

chime chime chime

our Nandini cow.

the Thai the Thai

my sister's anklets.

knom knom knom

train at the outer station.

nim nim nim

worshipping mother.

that terrible alarm clock again

trongggggggggggggggggggggg.

My heart beats

lub dub lub dub.

Cling cling cling

my wife's bangles.

I wake up to the

world of sounds.

Those twin cities

Lightning, thunder, torrential downpour,
was going on around the world.
No one had any idea what to do about it.
a dissolving fluent world,
cruelty was streaming in minds.
Egoistic egocentric decisions
for a one-up programme.
Men always leave some seed of discord
to fight about it later!

Peace and tranquillity depleted,
children do not play anymore.
Birds and animals retreated to self-exile.
Rain was heavily deluging the minds.
The gruesome frantic dance is in full swing.

The fight continues on the land
where Buddhism is a living philosophy.

The rain stopped for a while.

Children and women went out with a sigh.

Suddenly there was a mushroom sprout in Hiroshima!

Overnight the city tremor,

and all turned into ashes

charred remains of life heckled

showed wry faces at humanity.

Then there was another mushroom

Nagasaki trembled like Pompeii.

People in the city frostbit.

the Nuclear winter consumed the limbs

of life

limbless babies were born there as a curse

to human beings

Hiroshima and Nagasaki

we lower our heads in shame

we lower our heads in shame

the entire world bows down at your feet

still, Buddha smiles#

for whom?

* Buddha smiles is a code word given for India's nuclear
programme

Four seconds

On this day we met on a celestial dais

you were emitting a glow of freshness

God had decorated you with splendour

were sprinkling aroma of your grace

your elegance vibrated all over the floor

eyes wide open I admired your pulchritude

I noticed a beauty spot on your dimple was smiling

you were introduced to me by the destiny

when I took your hand you were vibrating my soul

time we spent together were moments of ecstasy

we showered silky flowers of love in veneration

ending up tying our nuptial knot on a heavenly day

Four beautiful years have passed like four divine seconds

I still hear the sweet soft chimes of your soul in mine

If I say I love you would be a cliché

I am yet in search of words to express my feelings

Thank you for making four years into four lively seconds

Fear

Time is galloping in rhythmic hoofing

I wonder where am I in this cosmic theatre

I stretch my little hands to reach my mother

I am hungry, tired and thirsty for her love

in the maze and haze of the universe, I tremble

with a slowly consuming fear, I watch the eclipse

Hold time

Every tick that echoes in my heart reverberates in my ears.

Every second that has gone is stale and never will be back.

the day I was bone has gone behind me, and become a history of time.

From moment to moment, I trek to an infinity of unknown realms.

Every cell that was born with me has changed or dead,

not the same anymore.

Unaware my life floats in the hands-on unknown

I try to stop the pendulum, only to tumble down the cliff

finally was consumed by the eternity of mighty time

who can escape the stronghold of time?

Silent smile

Burn you

with a tongue of fire

smell the flower of flesh

while exploring the tunnel of love

saw your silent smile

Soapsuds

In the infinite ocean of the universe

he plays with a bubble blower.

Under the arch of creativity

soapsuds float carried by currents.

Galaxies dance to tunes.

Divine theme music plays softly.

Sky, planets, moons, stars, suns,

all float in streams of the milky way.

My colourful dream vanishes,

fell off the cot to reality.

He moves his magic wand

Lo, nothing exists in a deluge.

He floats beyond space and time

having his last laugh.

Thank you, Jesus

A great thought takes birth

my soul gets blessed

an ecstatic effulgence

flood over my body

I remember your sacrifice

for humanity

wearing a thorny crown

then you bathed us

in the divine blood of purity

Thank you my beloved Jesus

we are liberated

to Freedom

Mannequins

Imagination by thoughts,

words and sounds

men experimented

his fantasy

It is one of the gifts

gifted by the grace of god to humans

history is hidden under

obesity of facts

fossils of life are compressed

in between obscurity and time

with a toothbrush

historians decipher

shells of existence

out of curiosity

they excavate curios

for our museums and libraries

fancy of creativity

took men to outer space

and planets

geography of imagination

sleeps in the dreams of mind

great fascinating men

wrote their dreams

in all forms of literature

we put our vision

to life in words

fancy made script

with mind's eyes

we wrote our colourful

images of life forms in text

milked art forms

from the udder

of imagery

aesthetics took shape

from the fertility of

minds

there the contours

of species manifested

like mannequins

displayed

in the brain cells,

is reproduced

in the canvas of time

I guide myself

I was floating

my thoughts are in disarray

mind heavy

I was pushing myself

thrashing my shade

crushing my mind

my body lose

hand and legs

rattling

I vomit my Gambrinous emotions

with a messy unsteady tongue

I guide myself

into the pit of a gutter

fallen there asleep

Allure of life

Spring arrives with all its splendour

earth soaked with monsoon rains

takes a deep fresh breather

the smell of earth fills the nostrils

life moves slowly from cuddled laziness

sun shower colours on flowers

every nook and corner bloom

trees adorned with fresh silky sprouts

creepers dance with flowers

the roadside is carpeted with fresh blooms

shower the aroma of nature on passers-by

butterflies and seasonal birds all arrive

a piece of heaven falls on the earth

like the vibrant weather, women come out

fine-tuning with nature they dance

in streaming soft sweet steps

It is a pleasure burst from the heart

mind body and thoughts merge

invoking frozen idols to life

children also join in creating

a pattern of images from their mind

time stands still observing the allure of life

Curse of time

As a reminder,

For the season

When dogwoods blossom

The blessings arrive

From heaven.

In cross-shaped flowers,

The corolla formed

As crucifix.

With nail holes,

Holy blood stains

And a thorny crown

At the centre

Is a replica of the cross

He carried

Made of dogwood.

Curse of time

made the wood

Thin in history.

Let us weep

shamelessly

for him

who wore our sins

As crown

And still, help us

Cross the river of Hades

To reach heaven

Sunburned

Heatwave

melting me down.

Dehydrated

thoughts.

My muse is

sunburned.

Sun drains

the water holes.

Unending wait

for summer rain.

Strung together

Everything in this cosmos

is linked by a unique thread

of uniting imagination

every being and non-being

exists related to one another

stringed together as beads

connected by a magic faith

life is expected to revolve

in an escalator as a cycle

hopes to move us forward

despite fear and pain of

death and birth

Nine expressions

There are many moods of the sea.

Sometimes it has amour

It invokes the expression of lovers on shore.

In another mood, it displays a comic.

Philosophers take life as a comedy.

Extremely pathetic when it watches poor

who sit on her shore and weep silently

for a morsel

It turns furious and shows a frantic dance

a tantrum, when she is worried

about depleting her image.

She worships heroism when heroes face

arrive on her beach.

Sometimes she turns terrible with

uncontrollable tsunami trees.

Occasionally she built odious

mountainous waves, spreading her

matted hair on the shore.

Wonderstruck surrealist painter

kept nine ornated frames to

paint her nine expressive faces.

Just watch her closely for a long time,

meditate on her serenity, listen to her

chant AUM

peace, calm, and happiness will dawn

the mind will be free like the children

on the beach.

You might leave a tiny footprint

of your own on her lap of magnanimity

Like billows

Like billows

CARESSING the FIRES

BODY BURNS

with a desire to

fly away to the

heaven of hell.

FINGERS move

touching the EDGE

PUMMELING

of a weeping SPOT,

sliding cliff of a

HEATED matchstick

BUILDS ecstasy bubbles

produce SCREAMS

of BUBBLING joy.

BREATH stops GASP

for a while.

The FLESH of roseate lips

GLISTENS with

discharge of love potion,

OVERFLOWS ME.

RUBBED bruised SKIN

seeks the pleasure of pain.

Ecstasy MOANS

PANTING heavily.

I WHIMPER with

SWEAT and TREMBLE.

while craving

for the smell of my man.

Divine molecule

In the magnanimity
of time and space,
there is webcasting.

Spider is waiting
spread with a magnificent
the silky-threaded web.
It is decorated with
globules of time machines.

Heads are rolling
with the minutes and
hour hands.
Lives are ticking
by seconds.

Like a magician
the spider pulls

threads to entangle

the traps.

The world is trapped

in the time net.

Like a disappearing act of magic

the netted world

appears and disappears

as and when the net

is pulled on and off.

In the absence of a net,

time stands still.

sleep dissolved

with eternity.

Nothing remains

except

the sound of silence!

Until time gets up to another dream

with a cosmic dance, by the hum

of the divine molecule

AUM

My mind

From the mystery of time

I was born with a lot of causes and effects.

As a newborn, I had a zero mind

I lived in the hands of my forlornness.

Fear struck me every moment

I sought comfort in the warm bosoms of my mother.

I grew up slowly into a girl

then into a young lady with wide eyes

looking into the world with wonder.

I kept a veil of shyness in my mind.

then I craved for love, a manly love.

grew into a woman without

any shyness or fear.

The world taught me the mystery of life.

My mind was stuffed and stiff

with a lot of junk and fallouts.

I stared at myself and found

a monster in my mind with fearful shades.

found a giant frog ready to leap out

to freedom from the stuffy stinky mind

A pauper of dreams

Like a glow-worm

I walked all over

emitting an aura,

flew as a firefly,

showing tiny light

to the sun and moon!

light to the world.

Time put a lid on me

a manhole cover

I went down

into the black hole of time

asphyxiating

unwept, unsung.

A pauper of dreams

6/11/26/11/26/1126/11

My speech was dead in my throat.

My words are stagnant in my pen.

My thoughts were frenzied, deranged.

I am afraid to recollect scenes.

As the day goes by, they add on lies.

mongering war for Vulture's feast.

Still, they live in an era of Gory,

Attack all around as Ghazni.

Spitting bullets on innocents,

Terror (jihad) in the name of religion.

Bled we lie on an arrow bed.

Composed we fold our hands.

A Sad smile on the face is not cowardice.

It is a divine glow of our courage.

Blood decked, turned bloody flowers.
Hibiscus blooms in every heart.
With blood stains, sunrise every day,
until perpetrators are punished.

A nation of making believers
loves to dance in the holocaust.
Their leaders spit hate on freedom,
Wearing a turban of indecency

We just wish to say a prayer for all,
By lighting a candle in our hearts.
My tears flow incessantly until then,
those fallen flowers are consecrated

Summer blue moon

A dream fell on her pallet.

A lump of the azure sky with stars.

She mixed it with the grace of her thoughts,

started to paint a portrait.

After some strokes with her magic brush

the painter entered into the canvas.

The sketch got alive and started moving,

as she breathed life into it.

With a soft caress, she filled blue

became one with the painting,

mixing her soul.

It was a timeless, infinitely eternal

portrait of life's mystery

she named it 'summer blue moon

Nothing but the truth

At last,

you are telling

the truth

nothing

but the

truth.

Life to dead words

The poet breathes life into dead words.

Adorn it with sweet diction and cadence.

Decorate more with diamonds and pearls

She walks on the ramp as a beauty queen

555 *State express*

He used to come with

Five golden teeth glowing widely

Wristed with a golden watch

showed rings on five fingers

pretending unaware of the wear.

Lifted fingers like piano keys

showed off his net worth

often lifting his ray ban.

Masquerading he arrives suited well

profoundly sweating under the summer heat.

Yet he wears a suit

just to show off position.

Years back he too migrated

in search of a job.

The MiddleEast welcomed him as a houseboy.

Came back with a bang

emitting strong scented cheap cologne.

Now he needs a wife

looking for an educated girl

visited houses of young girls.

He wearing bell-bottomed outdated pants

And a cheap red tee shirt

holds keys to the marriage market!

Finally, marries a doctorate girl

holding a 555 state express.

I have a colour

I have a colour

colourless

colour

my entity

is lost

in that

hue

To capture the timid time

Timidity is balancing on the edge
of foolishness.
Time stands still with folded hands
unconcerned.
The stillness of the pool is inviting
a splash of an event.
Fall comes striking the very base
of tranquillity.
When the time starts ticking again
sure there will be a touchdown.
Maybe a severe tumbledown
a deluge of water overflowing
scene and frame.
Any moment she would be a frog
floating or leaping?
Only a secret eye is waiting to
capture the timid time through the peephole.

When I write

When I write

I need my words dug deep from

my soul

It just remains understood

becomes a chant of my heart

when I use my head

to ink, it becomes an absurd theatre

misunderstood to misinterpret

Symphony of life

The lone voice is the voice
that is heard, listened carefully
the uniqueness of the sound
attracts the attention of the mob.

All those great men were special
who back walked from the crowd
yodelling a clear clever tongue twister
Nobody can imitate it.

But they sang a soulful song
mixing with the tune of the music
captured the entire mode of tapping feet.
The world without multitude is dry
a monotony of communistic dreams.

If the world is having only one writer

who will read his work of art?

Variety is the core cause of creativity

creation arrives from the fertility of multiplicity.

The genesis of aesthetics is born out

from the soul of magnanimity.

Masterpieces took the birth from

a multi-faceted mind of imagination

Let birds be singing sweet melodies

but let the raven too, sing his songs!

The beauty of the world is a manifestation

of all beings and nonbeing together

conducting a soulful symphony of life.

Let there be many artists live under one roof

the roof of the artistic opera house.

Flower of love

When I talk to you In a language

that I can express only by the urge of my sensuality.

I want your response with the fire of your tongue.

Let me enter your tunnel of volcanic eruptions

and merge in the honeydew flower of love.

City Of Pompeii

Once

Before the doomsday

It was fun and frolics

For Children of Chernobyl

Quiet and happy

They waded freely

in the ocean of fun.

Merry go round of the time

jumping on the toy horse tops

Had whale of a time
In the carnival of rides.

Suddenly howl of sirens
blaring alarms,
the city grinds to a halt.
Schools closed
shops shutters down
people ran for shelters.

A fire-spitting dragon
flashes through the streets
charred remains on both sides.
The heat wave of radiation
strikes the city halls
children run in fear.
Helpless cry looms everywhere
mothers weep for help.
While watching the scenario
they found their children
stop crying.
Found them fizzle out

melting down in a puddle

their rattling bones

lie scattered.

They were covered

in the ashes of arrogance.

Remain as cruel jokes of rulers!

Monuments of Chernobyl

remain as

the modern disaster like

Mount Vesuvius

the city of Pompeii!

Jingle of love

The wind was humming a tune.

The music lying in my soul awoke

I became a flute, emitting celestial songs.

My vocal cord became strings.

Mind fine-tuned a cosmic rhythm.

Thoughts streamed as melody

flowed out as drizzling tones.

Fingers keyed the rhymes of love

every cell danced with the tempo

the moonlight outside moved with the wind

like a wave kissing the shore

I flowed as a stream of delight

as stars were winking at each other.

Silhouette of light and shade

creates a rhythmic symphony

I dream walk dreaming a rhapsody

drumming my thoughts slowly.

Under the night drizzle of rain

I drench in ecstasy.

My heart beats a jingle of love

Author notes:

Write a poem for contest Rhapsody on a Windy Night T S Eliot
Contest

I love T S Eliot's poetry. What I would like you to do for this contest
is use the poem Rhapsody on a Windy Night, and produce your
poem in the style of this great poet. I am offering big points for this
contest so would like to read your poems in the style of this poet. I
DO NOT want a rewritten version of the poem Rhapsody on a windy
night; rather what I'm looking for is YOUR interpretation of this
poem. So have a go and see what you can come up with. Remember I
am offering big points for this so have a go. You may use whichever
style you choose in your submitted work. I don't mind any longer
writing but please no paradise lost submissions. Any questions feel
free to message me. Enjoy the contest and have fun

Wide net

The tree of life emerges

from the deluge of time.

The whole universe is created

In the womb of desires,

while the hood of lust

climbs to the trunk of sensuality.

Ecstasy creates a heaven

spreading the tentacles

to the wide net of creation!

The flesh of the moon

Leftovers, spills,

sediments of yesterday.

Crushed rose petals

The bleed

of lipstick on the forefront.

I remember your,

emotion-filled screams.

Your body smell

on my lips and nostrils.

I can see your thirst

your qualms about.....

We wanted to explore more

I saw the wink of the moon

stars settle for a nightcap.

Found you melting down.

The flesh of the moon

was floating lazily in the pool

I placed a parting kiss

smearing on my lips

your lust and blood

Merge

Intoxicated
she lies flat on the
chest of nature.
Her long hair
spread wildly on earth.

Breathing slowly
she became a wildfire.
Flames eating away
the wilderness of the forest.
Danced with
with the hurricane.

Unfolded her
slowly into the
manly hands
of powerful emotions.

Screaming

away her desire

she

melted down

while joining the estuary.

Merged

in the extreme.

Tranquillity of silence

Waves and heaves

stopped

abruptly.

She slept in peace

unaware of her body

consciousness.

Burden of life

He was born in the marshland of life.

The burden of his past still haunts him

The vulture of fate carries him away,

into distant lands of birth and death.

He is being eaten away by the beaks of fate,

torn away the flesh of desires bit by bit.

The wild cry for help is not heard anywhere,

because time is consuming him to destiny.

The entire chain of life is witnessing

as nature bleeds to death in the hands of time.

Laws of nature will have a run of their course

until such time the burdens are no more.

Life is a fantasy

Through the flow of time

We exist as a tiny insignificant

Constellation

Each atom is arranged perfectly

Discharging its functions in order

The entity of galaxies lives as a dream

Of a magnificent design

The world is created as fantasy unlimited,

Unfinished.And untold.

Is there anything that survives here

are not fantasies?

The precision of revolving planets

The laws of nature

Eternal laws of birth and death

I rejoice to watch the rainfall, the music

Of rain

The murmurs of fall

The warmth of summer

The tan on my skin

The frozen meditative mind of winter

The smile of spring

Even your ecstatic smile is a fantasy for me

Let me live on this fantasy ever!

The food was not served

The host invites

for a feast

you dress up

the best of

your dinner jacket

seated at the dinner table

the banquet is

on

but

The food was not

served

The fantasy of a dream

Once in my dream, an angel came.

She took me on her wings,

beyond seas, sky, and galaxies.

She put me in a gown of soft sky silk,

adorned me with rare gems.

Placed a crown studded with stars.

half moon on the side.

We floated across the blue sky,

pushed white puffy clouds to the side.

Visited fairy lands n' plucked

passion fruits and drank ambrosia of love.

She taught me how to fly without wings

we giggled and laughed girly smiles!

Unaware I opened my eyes

I was lying on the floor with a thud.

Splints of my laughter lie scattered on the floor
flints of dream litter around

I found a feather in my pillow
smiling and tickling my nose!

 Sun is retiring to the west bed
Sun is retiring to the west bed
his sleepy eyes slowly closing
the world is tilting towards night,
as he carries the globe along.

Soon the lights will open their eyes
before the retreat, he looks
to the world once more to see
his reflection on the lake
where the images sleep.

He is the only painter
who create masterpieces daily,
every moment.
with a stroke of his brush.
Awestruck I ink my thoughts here

Waiting

Thoughts bleed profoundly
Fear rules the sky of the mind
Clouds of insecurity
Roam lazily unable to settle
In the partying crowd of
Planets and stars
He stands alone with a Grimm
A fast-approaching storm
Dark clouds assemble
Thunderbolt, lightning,
Threatening a showdown.
The moody sky touches down
Crimson rain shall fall anytime
Soon rivers of sorrow will flow
In between the earth trembling
Who will retrieve the orphan
From the deluge of destiny
My thoughts get dried in the pen.
Waiting for the verdict.

I offer a tempest

I have a deep sense

of freedom

to offer you with

the softness of my charm

invoke you into my

wild nature

invite to explore

the depths of

of my unquenchable

thirst for your

manliness

I offer you, my

slavery

my subtle

un sprout desires

to be kneaded

kindled
enough
to respond to
the strength
of your passion

I offer all
my nature bloom
to get merged
in the heat
of blazing sunlight

I would shine
after you
as a shadow
of your manhood.
I offer you
my feminine
hurricane
to consume
you are in the tempest
of our lovemaking

When the object fades away

There is a shadow follows everywhere

as long as light lives shades have a life to live

the pain and pleasure are unaware by the silhouette

it just moves through the seasons unaffected at any time

it just observes the happenings unmindful of dirt or stink

It has a pure identity of its own and goes on and on

shadow dances to the tune of your rhythm

and retires into the oblivion when object fades away

The book on fire

When the world around suffers

handcuffed, chained, to slavery

Helplessness, frustration

children suffer from hunger

poverty, illness

dictators, autocrats, corrupt

politics

then there comes a messiah

rises from the ashes like a phoenix

with wings and a heart of fire

somewhere from the obscurity

a pen filled with the ink of fire

arises

writes the emotional essay of life

and death

every word that is linked, inked

to a stream of fire

burns

the reader gets up with a torch

dances frantic

burns into a towering inferno

destroying in the deluge

melted rocks flow as lava

the hidden anger

of the society

A tornado of revolutions

sweeps the world

the firepower of a book

is enough for a renaissance

to become a monument

of human history

the book is on fire!

Her ponytail

A beautiful azure screen

of nature

where every moment

aesthetic creations

are created

in exotic tones and colour

No one has

seen the depth of it

in the power of windy

of whirlpool

matters take birth

an un-scalable

mystery

surrounds like a mystic puzzle

her ponytail

knotted with a rainbow

Entangled in the rhythm

Souls communicate
with the egos of the body

a beautiful dawn
with the warmth of the sun
cool aromatic mist
envelopes
drizzling
golden granules

happy tears roll
on the cheeks of dreams

glitters
millions of stars
wink at
the Casanova moon,

dance with

then kiss the unique soul.

Exchange

bubble gums

passion sticks

on the lips

unable to part

entangled

in the rhythmic

breathe.

It is a pause

It is a pause

a posture

a lioness's review

into path

she had trekked

there are many

uncountable

imprints

in a mess of

footprints

yes she takes

coffee break

reminiscing

her life

and her beloveds

the queen looks

at the moon

howls

exalted

If my thoughts are real?

My words turn stale

meaningless to describe you

as you are beyond

meanings, shapes and sounds

yet I try to string you

in a capsule of worthless sounds

You are a flow of the subtle song

streaming into the depth of awareness

Often making an experience of bliss

the music in between life and death

as you sing it becomes real

you are sleeping

in the petals of a dream

sleepwalks

into an exotic world

of fantasy

dances through the souls

stare through the eyes

of a curious child

You become

princess of nature

donning the gown

of colourful corollas

the lady strolls

into the wide world

each sound reverberate

from the heart of love

you are in it

delving as a divine queen

making the world sleep

in your lap of timelessness

Just sing for me alone once

caress my hair

fondle my thoughts

make me sleep in the cradle

of your lullaby

I just saw you dancing

with wolfs

grinding stars and the moon

your gown was

twinkling with stardust

then I saw you floating

with the dead moon

and stars

holding hands of embrace

Just a drop of tear for her

No one ever sheds a drop of a tear for her

Nobody remembers her sacrifice

Life was pregnant in the womb of time

she was a fireball melting her inside out

then one day she cooled her thoughts

life was born from the infinity of mystery

A divine molecule took shape of a man and woman

we grew into a mass of circumstances

controlled every object and creature on earth

made them slaves for the benefit of craves

exploited mother stampeded with a hoof of selfishness

rode our stallions raising dust and fumes

ploughed, dug, tilled, mined the bowels

like a cow, we sucked her milk until the udder bled

dumped our filth and garbage

suffocated with plastics, chemicals, pesticides

Never said a word of thanks for her sacrifice

Now her face is dark with carbon dioxide

disfigured limbs with acid rains

she is burning herself with ultraviolet radiation

yet she never says a word against

she is the mother of all

Mother Earth is an embodiment of grace

In the cuddle of imagination

I became a sculpture

kneading the soft clay

with my feather fingers

chiselled and carved you out of my soul

filling your curves with

my careful fondle of love

created every cell of your body

with caress

invoking you from the depth

of desires

My hands danced

with your tenderness

pressing the fantasy

from a sleeping hurricane

Moved my lust into

the bliss of your love

flaming each tissue

of your elegant figure

measured length and breath

of shape

with the lips of my craves

I hugged tightly

to the tenderness of love

creating a beauty

out of my lust

we moved on the

wings of ecstasy

to a heaven

we built together

in the cuddle of our imagination

A blissful twilight

An angel lost her wings
pushed her down to oblivion

she had a feather
a flint of a light
from the crown of the moon

searching for
the lost quill
her body was covered
with the moonlit

transparent details of
heaving waves
of love and passion
flowered on her skin

she became a bloom

of a night

queen of darkness

emitting fragrance of

a blissful twilight dawn

Bearing the fruits of my sin?

The full bloom flower

manifests magnanimity

graced by pulchritude

soft subtle hue drizzles allure

the dawn had arrived

in splendour

beauty pervades all though

earth

I had been waiting for

with a bit of hesitation

a lot of anxiety

at last the butterflies

came, the street Romeos

then the honeybees

with an irritating buzz

pierced their dirty feelers
I was horripilate
thinking that he would
snatch my virginity
nothing happened
he went away to another
beauty bloom

then came the Beetle
he had that horrible eyes
and hot biting lips
and those dark stingers

I was mad at him
he embraced my soft
subtle emotions
held me tight under his
dark hairy arms
kissed me to heaven
tore my emotions
my silky petals
wounded me badly

took my Honey

my pollen

Until I realized

happenings

turned into

a faded sweating

boiling nymph

I was unpacked

as slave

I was not destroyed

But loomed into a full flora

bearing

the fruits of my pleasant pain

Motherly

Brooding over the eggs of warm hopes

I created my little wishes

It was tickling with life by the celestial grace

I visualized being on the top of the world

becoming a mother in the mass of time

carried my life safely until this moment

he had me under the fold of his wings of protection

we enjoyed warm emotions giving

birth to the siblings of our life

I watched each treasure under my wings daily

anxiety touched shells of my thoughts and felt each moment a
lengthy aeon

I could feel each movement inside the membrane of life

One golden day the first shell cracked making way for my
little duckling, at last, all of them came out of divine shells

I watched those little pink beaks, unsettled tiny wings

it was the day of my life I gave my little ones the first feed of
worms

they grew, now freely roaming as my dreams

But children, be careful of each step you take

there is always a danger in the kerb

watch be safe don't become a dressed duck on their dinner
table!

She became

Pushing back the streams
she swam across
to the land of fantasy

discarding her teen
turned into a dream herself
possessed by spirits
of youthfulness
ready to taste the
goodness and sourness

nature nurtured her
with the elegant
innocent beauty

she turned into a flame
ready to burn

the hearts of men

Masquerading
with an inflicting smile
she became
the queen of many hearts

one day she
matured into Cleopatra

Smell of life

I frame my thoughts

near the window pane

with a view to

the ambience of serenity

every object

captures my brush

of words

in a pallet of colours

in the silence

of exotic unique

colours

my easel meditates

as my minds

creates a collage

of real world

In my dream sketches

I talk to her

silently

dancing with

her nudity

emitting smell

of earth

Mother Earth

The time just peeped into his soul
invoking his celestiality
music, rhyme and rhythm
propped the vibrato of his music
he sang and danced the world
to the tunes of his lyrics
gliding on a rainbow
he stepped on the podium
moon walked along with the crowd

One day he sang
the melody of his life
from the depth of astral spheres
he touched and tapped his feet
softly on the soil
the sand and sea
he became singing a medley
a folklore
the song divine mother earth

Veil of silence

I am pedalling my thoughts
In words of anxiety
Not so sure of the next moment
and the words that come out of my pen

Like a Frog, I stare and watch with roving eyes
the silent pond mediates
the stillness of the night

stars and the moon dive into
the depth of my pond
Lotus leaves move smoothly
along the breeze
eyes closed Lotuses

pelting a stone onto the darkness
I listen to skipping notes
the frog in me leaps across

a splash and flash into the lake

veil of reticence

covers my musing

A moment of bliss

Slowly she strolls in

there she is in a robe of white

a sprinkle of glow, a smile so sweet

murmur drops to pin-drop silence

her hands move on both sides

touching the mob in a row

a cute baby jumps onto her

she carries her in her arms

they smile at each other kissing

the proud baby looks around

as if she is riding a chariot of love

by a rolling look around the crowd

she grabs each one in her vision

sending grace of her platonic love

making each one in the assembly a child

she sings a spiritual lullaby

making each one dance in ecstasy

joins the dancers at the height of devotion

and the baby in you is invoked

dreaming in bliss we all sleep

in the lap of meditation

I was hooked by a desire

Here I come often

with fishing line and hook

It is my golden pond

I see the sun taking

a dip

his blond hair shining

sometimes I found him taking a nap

on the flaxen sand

silently I watch the hook plunge

looking for the goldfishes

hooking my dreams I wait

in the serenity of silence

feeling each pulse of ripples

my thoughts flow along fishline

suddenly

there is hope

I pull the line

So there

a splash

I was hooked by a desire!

Until

The shadow of karma

follows

the day of your birth

as we move with delusion

dark shade consumes the life

fear,

gloom covers the body.....Until

Filling the corolla of life

It was a blue drizzle

making music of sanctity

In the serene lake of the mind

the rise and fall of ripples

composes a rhythm

a melody on the satin turf

holding her veil of shyness

she flowed in, Lotus bloom

her wide blue eyes

looking at the world with ecstasy

spreading the aroma of her exotic complexion

with silky pink petals

opening slowly to the vastness

filling the air with a subtle fragrance

she takes a dip in the lake of my mind

horripilate my senses

Shades of blue satin seep into the lake

beads of pearl cascade over her hair

she comes out with a smile of the universe

as the sun pushes the veil of mist

to expose her pulchritude

I see her dancing

on the lotus intoxicated

by nature

a breeze carries her along

filling the corolla with life

That is life

The World

a podium set for a drama

all are actors

from microbes to man

nonbeing being stage properties

orchestra is on

fiddling strings of life

vibes of drum

seventh symphony

the conductor

circles his baton

and begins the concert

a roar of animals

singing birds

open air theatre is live

all wear different

masks

to the script of the director

the prompter is behind

running the show

tap dancers on the floor

each one

enacts the role

and discard costumes

at the end

comedies tragedies

tragic comedies

monologue dialogues

the scenes change

vibrates to the cosmic rhythm

that is life

Love never gives up

She was drowning

in a whirlpool of darkness

he dived

with a torch of confidence

in the nucleus of the current

they lived

surrounded by a tornado

they survived

bound together

in compassion

Wand of magnanimity

Yes the perfection

in every creation

masterly engineered

products

But why some

some got truncated

on the final product

some defective

were you doing over time?

No, I know you are not

it is your desire

to make a unique

statement

an output of your

special skill and care

Those shortfalls are

not yours

it is your wish

to give those children

your special hand

of compassion

and a pointed finger

to humanity

to take care of the

beauty you have

created on them

We, humans, do not know

your wish

I am sure those

are your special

wonder kids

making us

aware

to take care of

our duty

in action

Oh God give us

the strength

to rear those folks

on a bed of roses

protect

our dignity by

making our feelings

as your kindness

Just act

through us, our hand

with a magic

wand of magnanimity

We know you will

make every being

an instrument of your

engineering

Bonfire of constitutions

Now the atmosphere is shrinking

stenchy with sycophancy around

a storm is brewing somewhere

the stage set for a puppet show

the puppeteer holding the lines

what a man he is with a suit

costly casual golden threads

smell burning the constitutions??

Long journey

Word on word

I travel when I read

book to book

discover new lands

I never saw

to the utopia

sound to sound

melody to melody

yes to the magic of music

imagination carry me

over seven seas

to the deserts of Rajputana

and deserts of California

I listen to singing sands

symphony of waves

cradle to the coffin is a long tour

from wishes to wishes

dreams to dreams I trek

one day

I close the travel bag

writing a travelogue of my life

A silent explosion

From the chaotic battlefield,

a whole world of horribly terrible noises

cry of fear, pain and death

shells and bullets crack

splinters fly past

one moment it is all there

the deafening

then

ears go blind!

a slow-motion movie

the heaviness falls silent

like a feather everything floats

thunder and lightning ends

world of voice and names

disappear

vision hangs

meaningless muteness

comes alive

into meaningful silence

Names and forms vanish

in the completeness of

divine soliloquy!

you are one with

a silent explosion

into the infinite stillness of time

Negligee

I am

wearing

my wife's

soft perfumed

negligee

since she left

me in a huff.

where ever

she is

let her be happy

with her new lover!

Pity

her if she is not

Invisible impressions

In the crowd

out of the world

I have a room with a window

opening to outside

a view of the world

squatting in a corner

on a rocking chair

the soliloquy monologues

flow. a flowchart of life

often I dive deep into the thoughts

entangled

in the labyrinth

unaware of the assembly

aimlessly I move

as a sheep

biting to the taste

the smell and sweat of life around

rock incessantly

communicating in silence

often fly over

as a superman

viewing the reality

later retire to my corner

with a mind full of emotions

to sketch

yet my walls are empty

with invisible

impressions

write something in my

visitor's book

as to what you see in my nook

and empty mute corner

Off my soul

A chisel in my pen

carved out

my fantasy

as a lady

you

manifested

as sculpture

of my soul

a fine mural

exhibit

Awaiting

Once they were full

filled with texture and taste

aromatic colourful

creams and pickles

beverages

tasty yummy

testifying the imagination

of the creator

got emptied

consumed bit by bit

before the expiry date

later

got stuck

spent force

grey

human jugs, jars

and bottles

in all shapes litter

dirty, dusty living

at the mercy

lie watching windowsills

some become scarecrows

rest awaiting the junkyard truck!

You and me

Dredging my thoughts

found you hiding

in the oblivion of time

ploughing through

discovered your fineness

flowers of your preaching

teaching

everybody forgot

what you have in mind

struck

your commandments

for humanity of

worthy beings

crucified

imprisoned you in the

altar

never let you out

speak in a sermon

when I mix my thoughts

always saw your cute little face

spreading on the palette

often you possessed my brush

created

unique portrait

of a universal baby

to be a sculptor on my canvas

breathed fresh air

into your nostrils

created you

in my shape

special colour schemes

reincarnated

resurrected

became you in me

me in your kingdom

Silence of freedom

I can hear that, the galloping white horse
hoofing freely in the dreamy fields inside

body mind and spirit entangled in the
labyrinth of untied ties
time runs away speedily
chained emotions chock

clarion calls one day the strings break
the mind jumps out, liberation
on the wings of newly found freedom
she floats glides lazily over the vastness of the magnificent sky
craving for a celebration of the newfound free spirit
higher up the blue sky merges into
imaginations spread, hover over different fairy landscapes,
ambience, continents, oceans mountains and valleys
among the vastness, I realise my tininess

as I dissolve in the silence of freedom! beautiful emancipation

From the crude darkening

From the crude darkening

messenger of hope risen

invoked the grace of divine

from the ancient mount serene

saw a rising star,

the lodestar to steer clear of the rough sea

into the light of freedom

surrounded by constellations

an index finger to hold on to existence

darkened faces took a breath

of relief and relaxation

horror-struck pupils

had the vision of a saviour

devils were ruling the masses

eating into the brains and sights

once the earth was hoofed

stampeded by giant creations like dinosaurs

all of them returned extinct

some got fossiled in the tunnel of time

often we humans mated our thoughts

with their cruelty

somewhere in the infinity, our DNA matched

hiding stuck our heads in a cloud of insecurity

we watered Daisies of hope

ploughed our lands

planted civilizations' renaissance and reformation

through deep penance, and mediation

acquired skills to hold the universe

a palmed bubble

incarnated the entire galaxies

in the palm of wisdom

our masters did that to guide us to the truth

one day we plotted in the last supper

to kill the golden goose

we did that for a few dollars more

Evolution

Wading through countless bodies

he reached the pinnacle of evolution

fine-tuning into a human being

who learned to laugh and smile

emote compassion, love and hate

expressed nine facial expressions of emotions

became a storyteller

wearing a theme in every thought

wore colourfully designed masks

was a child full of thrust

drank sour and sweet

quarrelled questioned and did a tantrum

a girl took him to another shore

there they lived and ate the apple

danced under floodlight
prayed and paused

fortunes came to them and children too
realised they are on a stage show
enacting a predestined script
changing face every time

time made folds of wisdom in disguise
looking far ahead into future
he discarded everything
his face had shocking memories

started untying his wrinkles
found himself. a sweet baby!
Ready to thrust again into another adventure
metamorphosis into the truth of his mission

A hermit

She swam across many oceans

braved the high sea mountainous waves

glided through the winds

dived into the abyss

met with many friends

sharks, whales

sea lions, horses

vegetation of weeds

dancing starfishes

reflection of the Sun, moons and stars

dancing with the waves

she was a mature female

with flesh and blood

emotions shaded on shells

decorated her with shades of a rainbow

many children born out of her love

reared them

taken them to the garden of coral reefs

she turned into a hermit

leaving her body

sought the serenity

meditated on the shore

listening to the primordial sound

echoing from her inner self

she lives the life of a saint

awaiting the divine lips

sound here

lift her as a monument

a mantelpiece decor

for the temple of heaven

We are all exposed

We are all exposed

our clothes are torn

doors are open

like a bunch of fools

we participate in social media

holding a gadget of self-destruction

the mobile phones

faceless facebooks

whats up

all the time we download

one app or the other

feed our brains with

junks of information

even governments are targeting

people

they remote control us

giving a Unique identification number

later identified as numeric

our bank balances siphoned

sim cards hacked

computer infected

control our life

feed us with fabrication

mine our habits

our interests

our likes and dislikes

they spook on us

our investments

we don't know what they are doing

they won't know what they are doing

we are trolled

pushed into techno slums

assembled our minds

to AI robots

sneak into privacy

feed us with jargon

we never know the language

gibberish syllables

seldom understood

one day

a guy comes driving a truck

and drive over an assembly

as we are watching

a robotic exhibition

Sprigs of hope

The scenery turns golden, and trees dressed in yellow

as Sun moves closer they shed their attire

a hot wave passes through

birds and animals try to take cover under their shadows, a
mirage hide and seek

water holes get dried, and rivers trickle desperately

dry grass rubs each other lighting a fire, the forest gets
charred, and sultry heat eats away the city.

poor citizens Sun stroked lives

humidity, dust and fumes, open-air cooking

the smell of burning tyres, humming air conditioners

where the elite hide from the heat

people sleeping on the terraces daring flies and mosquitos

then suddenly the eastern sky darkens elephants assemble
trumpeting, a sudden downpour

the flesh of a rainbow afloat

at last, the summer rain, the earth gets drenched in the thrill,
rain dance to celebrate

the happy melody rises in the air, new sprigs of hope

Dawn melodies

After the first chirp,

the rhythmic wave of music flows from infinity

a symphony for the arrival of the season

all birds join the chorus with Nightingale

in the theatre of dawn, they create a fusion

slowly waking from a deep slumber

keeping the remains of a colourful dream

in the eyes, the mind wanders through the window

The aroma of nature caresses my imagination

fresh sunlight kisses the petals of roses

with the shyness of a nuptial woman

she invokes the subtle flame of the sun

a spider is busy in the vicinity weaving silk

in my fantasy, I stretch myself to a fairyland

straddling the raw wilderness of nature

diving deep exploring into exquisiteness

found myself a child in the womb of time

suckling the nectar of love and wonder

oh, what an elegant beauty she is

Serenity again

Time lies ahead stretched

parallel lines meeting at infinity

always the train runs late

the anxiety of waiting ends

as the approaching whistle

shatter the silence of waiting

soon the roar of a cloud

hovering tornado arriving fast

a fearful sound of approaching engine

the tracks get thrusting vibes

flashing headlight

roaring steam and fume

crumbling sky

splash lights from compartments

grinding of breaks

red and green signals

the guard flashes his lantern

heavy downpour

people huddled on seats

their surrealistic emotionless faces move

a train of thoughts

heading to infinity

gale and bluster stops

serenity again

Thoughts flow incessantly

Thoughts flow incessantly

unending waves of the mind

anklets of rivulets giggle

making a whistling bugle

a chime tickles in the words

trickles in a fine drizzle

the tongue takes many turns

making my tunes in the throat

from the mystic realms,

lyrics take incarnation

wearing bangles and earrings

she dances to the divine tunes

sounds rhyme in melody

the magic of the muse invoked

nature merges with tempo

creating a lively fantasy

ink flows from heaven

articulating the ebb and flow of texts

I write about my inability

to conceive the wonder of aesthetics

my angel remains silent

invoking the beauty of nature

Only the one with

High elevation in thoughts

bountiful inexpressible joy

saturated happiness

flows everywhere boundless

the entire galaxies just rest in your palm

and compassion flows from the depth

to all beings and non-beings

good the bad and ugly all same

for the one who has seen it, experienced

love percolates and showered boundaryless

drenching micro to macrocosm

seer, scene and scene creator is the same

he floats on the wings of ecstasy

tears of happiness

face lit in the bliss of freedom

a thousand sunrise in him

as he falls into nature

rolling himself in the mud of identity

only the one with

In a frantic rhythm

It was all of a sudden

the hard golden disc had crashed

golden glow disappeared

somebody skyjacked the sun

there was no news about him

screen went blank

thousands of elephants on the rampage

tusks and trunks up

flashing the tails

the entire horizon was consumed

by the herd of wild bull elephants

trumpeting

spraying of water cannons

shouting screaming

god's own country was in the doldrums

earth was soaked to the brim

water levels raised

in all forty-three rivers in a frantic spree

they danced and danced

splashing high tides

filling mud and water in all the huts and palaces across

a deluge of time against human greed a lesson for a lifetime

In a frantic rhythm Part ii

A deep slumber took me to

non-existence

was on the soft petals of a dream

cool breeze

cuddling in the warmth

moved deeper into sleep

suddenly a nightmare

an assembly of

thousands of bull elephants

on the horizon

they are trumpeting

splitting the sky

the heart is restless

splashing their tails

raising their trunks

howling their tusks up
sudden the sky falls down
burst of clouds

raining with thundering

footfall

entire earth caved

landslides

doomed

flooded

a deluge of anger from rain gods

found my self-floating

with my wife on our bed

our furniture all afloat

elevated ecstasy

out sweet dream house

doomed nose deep

gasping for breath

I realised

that

one slight sneeze is enough

all to get submerged

in the tirade of nature

she was in excessive exuberance

dancing

in a frantic rhythm

pray stop it now

Aum Shanthi Shanthi Shanthi

Mother Earth

She stands there

watching the ebb and flow

much time the river was in high spate

bringing fertile soil to the shore

from time immemorial

much water had streamed out

before her eyes

sometimes flooded

became a stream of consciousness

high tides

low tides

reflections of life

many fishes lived inside her

rolling stones

ground to sand grains

she was witnessing it

many people have come

to this earth, lived here and left

civilizations flourished around the world

on the shores

where have all gone?

when was the first drop of water

became a part of the flow

there are many tombs

of memories built around

yet the river lives

before her vision all the time

and

she is a seer of the scenario

mother earth stands

erect viewing the

rise and set of the sun

her cheeks

invokes the shades

and the colours of dawn and dusk

Wink of a naughty boy

A scientist engineer

artist and painter

architect

he sketched, painted

mixed colours

from the realm of his gene

in his palette

drew the entire world

with his stencil pen

blueprints of centuries in advance

every being and nonbeing

imagined, visualised was created in

anatomic precision

all the walls

became his canvas

the frames of the renaissance

sculptured men and women

created with perfection

through anvil of mastery

hammered to fullness

painted the ceilings of divinity with

exotic brilliant hues of clouds

angels winged down

to watch him

choreographed rhythm

of his aesthetics

through Monalisa

Leonardo smiles at the

world

wink of a naughty boy

Let me snap shoot you

On a sleepless night

I saw you streaking

in the sky

amongst the stars of the day

you moved swiftly

from west to east

exposing

your full moon body

stretching your macho muscles

was it, not a sight for star-eyed

teenage girls

you gymnastic

six pack was rolling

in a sky show

reflecting in the sea

and mermaids

danced in emotional enchantments

waves of the deep ocean

touched the sky

kissing you

you made headlines

making people stare

through the balcony

let me snap shoot you

Attachment

I fell silent at your feet

Un-aware prostrating

Submitting myself helplessly

before the stunning enchanting beauty

remaining unconscious

being intoxicated I mumbled

chants of solitude from my depth

rooted in desperate pain

grew me as a vine

entangling and embracing you

wildly spreading deeper into your grace

invoking the warmth

of compassion

became a child

attached to the umbilical cord of divinity

with affection you guided me

Into realms beyond my imagination

suckling the Ambrosia of love

from your breasts, I grew in you as a disciple

spreading as fire burning my world away

as you lit my vision with effulgence

Tryst with nature

Slowly he painted

mixing unique textures

in his palette

brought out

brilliant colour combinations

merged his image

into the vastness of nature

flowed smooth

transcended

his body, mind and intellect

creating seasons

his thirst

lust for life

never ended

until he became

five elements

head the chant of life

the sun and moon

his eyes

rivers off blood vessels

his ears

space

stomach atmosphere

legs of action

hands of creation

fire groin

he became one with

truth

tryst with nature

chopping

his ear

My workshop

Often I retreat

into the wild blue yonder

searching for a workshop

where I chisel out my images

it is my dream house

I lit it with

my thoughts

worship my muse

with flowers of my words

invest her on a high pedestal

decked with velvet

lit a wick

dipped in the scented oil

burn an incense

fragrance would inspire

my creation

in the misty wonder, I float

slowly waving my wings

scooping mystery

from the universe

script my poem

from the suspense

of nothingness

tune my self

into the magic of

elevation

bliss of innocence

of a baby

Helpless in a whirlpool

A tempest is brewing

the head and tailwind strong

my boat is reeling

in a strong current

whirlpool opens its mouth

dark stars move fast

sky covered itself in a thick blanket

moon had disappeared

stars fell down the sea

along with horizon

hopes are nested in thoughts

children are playing

see my wife dreaming

good old days

we had watched the moon together

often his face changed
with our moods
watched her dark hair
fluttering in the breeze
kiss my beard

started rowing the boat
together
had our good and bad times
yet lived in the cuddle of hopes

wind is strong
soon it will be raining
mast is shaking
let me pull down
hands shiver
will I reach the shore
to be with them

tired I fell asleep
hands lose
oars cracking

lost my catches

skeletons are floating

where am I? am I dreaming?

remember some angelic wings

carried me across

hearing the familiar sounds

did I reach home? who rescued me?

My tiny feet

Yes a magic world folds

and unfolds

before the eyes

of words collected from

an exotic garden

arranged

oceanic waves caress the shore

blue water splash

splattering silver beads

sometimes

golden shadows rest

on the sand beach

a naughty breeze

encircles a lady sunbather

applying

sun lotion

tiny crabs walk around

placing their imprint

the painter

in the western sky

spills the paint

creating a sketch so unique

on the horizon

with these scribbles I sketched

my emotions

flash of

the imagery on the shore

of magnanimity

where master poets lived

I place where

my tiny feet

with fear

Shining dust of creation

Beyond galaxies

behind the universe

two magnificent eyes watch

from a high state of super intelligence

he holds a bubble of time

inside a beam skims

shining dust of creation

every being

nonbeings dive and swim as a mystery

from the altitude of realization

all becomes smaller than

smallest

bigger than the biggest

A Broader canvas

A full bloom horizon

beaming galaxies

glittery celestial decor

crystal rotating disco ball

emitting laser beams

an occasional flint of a thunderbolt

shaking the dance floor

I watch deep into the depth of

magic sky

mind delves deeper and deeper

scanning each star and planet

in the shell of an oyster

thoughts rest

meditating in solitude

I holding a sand canvas

twisting, turning, tuning the mind

Into fine images each moment

jumping into a stream of the milky way

holding the tip of a comet

I swing across

visioning a masterpiece

deposited on earth

sandstorm of imagination

moves hands of divinity in a sand canvas

Sheet of glass

The smell of good earth

virgin forest

doze off in the solitude

wilderness

keeps a serene silence

symphony of jungle

birds and animals

move in silence

unable to disturb the pulchritude

time meditates on the banks

watching the reflection in a flowing

sheet of glass

the grand trees

stand still stunned

at the elegance of nature

a dream unfolds

spreading a divine ambience

unaware

pen invokes sweet images

a poem from the cradle

of imagery

Raven with red eyes

A quick look at the pictures

of friends and, relatives

in the obituary page

shivering hands

thin fingers

wrinkles on skin

arthritis, knee pain

raven with red eyes

stare at you

From the depth

Gazing into the infinity

she invoked wilderness

thousands of murals formed her

image

the reflections of her mind

danced on her face as colour lights

her emotions swayed

on the psychedelic wings

her face shattered

into thousands of uniquely

pigmented corollas

turning herself into a melody

became a cosmic rhythm

engraved engrossed

In the depth of Rhapsody

she turned into a symphony

from the depth of her silence

streaming into the heart of divinity

Into a colour burst, she drizzled

mist of dawn

somewhere from eternity

flowed soft music from the violin

her beauty flows incessantly

through the sense of sensitivity

from the labyrinth entanglement of

coloured strings

I excavate you

invest you as an idol of my dream

let me delve deep

to find you

In me

The smell of paddy flowers

Anxiety is over

at last the first summer rain

she arrives at dawn

everybody is in deep sleep

the invigorating smell of earth

peacocks dance ecstatically

In the heart of each farmer

every family arrange

fresh fruits and vegetables on a display

for an auspicious dawn vision

at new year's eve

with a group, the farmers move to the fields

carrying the plough

and rushing the bullocks

worship the earth with an oil lamp

flowers and incense

move the furrow leading the bullocks

from the fertile memories

they sing a folk song in a colloquial

idyllic rhythm

they sweep through the time

and entire field tilled,

sow the seeds of hope in the paddy field

change of scenery

waves of silky green sprouts

farmers are busy weeding and manuring

hopes grow long

a soft subtle rejuvenating smell of flowers

slowly appears paddy bunches

turning the entire field into a golden trove

harvesting songs fill the air

happy villagers dance

the peasants fill the granary of happiness

until the next cycle

his sickle rests in his barn house

'Morally superior'

Still, the black hole of a well remains as a witness

in the garden

its protection wall struck with lead bullets

each one took a life of a poor man

who was there to celebrate the Baisakhi festival

Jawliyanwalah bagh became

a memorial of the freedom struggle

deep in the night,

the helpless scream of people

are resonated in the thoughts

General Dyer was an honourable man

whose army fired the thirsty bullets

an enthusiastic killer, who had no qualms

he enjoyed genocide

it says Rudyard Kipling donated

ten pounds for this mission!

feeble fearful faces thrilled him

was a happy man to kill unarmed people

who was asking the British empire

our birthright,- freedom

remember when they chopped the thumbs of

Indian muslin weavers

just to protect the cloth sales of Manchester

Gandhi replied to the greed with hand-spun Khadi clothes

that did the job

he made you bow down before

half-naked saint as you called humorously

were you not begging for a decent exit from India?

yes you did

general Dyer died unceremoniously

Michael O Dwyer fell

from a marked bullet from an unknown Sikh

nation demanded a wholehearted apology from Britain.

what we got was a Theresa mayhem

the moral superiority of our spirits

envelops your immaturity

as we live in a world of greedy

Ravens from the dark hole

flutter their wings of anger

yet, we send you the doves with an olive branch

Great! Britain the land of sunless Brexit domain

we are praying

for the departed souls of Jawliyanwalah bagh

on the occasion of

the hundredth anniversary of the martyrdom

The eternity of love

Time river flows incessantly
in the current of birth and death
life revolves in the whirlpool
gasping for breathing in the deluge
the flood came many times
washing away the evolutions
amoeba to woolly mammoths
ape to the man from the womb of time

many lives flooded through aeons
nothing remained forever
they all left in a huff of helplessness
trekked through the beaten path of love
strung with desires, dreams and attachments, possession,
nobody carried anything into the other world

ultimately

wise ones open up

they become saturated with bliss

one with effulgence

they embrace everything the good,

the bad, and the ugly

transcend this world entering into the

cosmic might of love

they tune into love eternal

concentrated compassion

the very nature of the mother

platonic love unstringed

let me embrace this universe

and into the eternity of love

Do not leave me ever

A prayerful vibration

all around the world

from the wisdom of my mother my master

may fragrant white flowers of peace and tranquillity shower
incessantly

like snowflakes of winter

tree rain of white blooms

all over the world from the sky

let serenity prevail everywhere

flowers ripple in all the oceans of the world

rivulets, rivers, and lakes stream full of milky blooms

mountains are white-capped with calmness

every flora and fauna is an adornment of peace

birds and animals are messengers of love

oh my Lord drizzle over me

your grace and love

hold me

do not leave me ever

Dream unfolds

Morning mist

the sun sends his first rays

golden granules dance

moon just glides back behind the horizon

faded litter of stars yet to hide

birds sing the dawn songs

morning theatre open

chants of Gayathri

daffodils smile

rose petals shine with diamonds

butterflies dance to the cosmic song

dream of nature unfolds

Nectar of love

Eyes wide open

a ray of hope

sun awakes

from the mud of the darkness

The lotus blooms

floating

fragrance spreads

inviting insects

to drink the nectar of love

Men and women buried

Men and women buried

in a tomb of desires

chained by taboos

under the cool delight of moonlit

they meet stealthily

floating on the wings of lust

in the wilderness of burning helplessness

they talk to each other

with the lips of prowess

they consume each other until dawn

Sand artist

Last week I visited the same beach same place

littered with cigarette buds

empty beer and Pepsi cans

innumerable footprints

I was becoming a sand artist

sculpturing her features

I created her combing the beach

like in a trance I chiselled her

an elegant creation of her feminity

I was meditative

a crowd had assembled around

suddenly lifting her veil she walked into infinity

I sleepwalked with my dream love

once I too was a Batchelor

lonely living in a den of ten people

to avoid the stench and smell of the room

spent my late evenings and Sundays on her lap

she had carried me away into the blue sky

On the crowded beach, I was alone

watching the depth of the vast horizon

talked to lone seagull lost falcon

highflying vulture

talked to stars and moon

circling planets

shrill tweaking parrots

I was dreaming a young dream

imagining imaging my future sweetheart

Dawn

A dream unfolds before my eyes
I was sleeping on a bed of rose petals
Floralyascenta's intoxicating smell
unknowingly I wound my hands around her

tweaking Tableauteniwink at the dawn
slowly she lifted the silky misty veil
the warm sun rays tickled her body
the world got up from shivering morning

Scootchminozi honking at the door
the thud of news paper and the clang of milk bottles
lazy steps leading to the front door
still, an ecstatic dream hangs over my eyes

far away Kafareedamin sounds the siren
blue-collar workers stream out of night shifts
their crumbled faces make Van Gogh's
we sit face to face with a steaming cup of coffee

Hugging saint

When the hugging saint visits your city

go and meet her

feel the pulse of god

smell of divinity

colour of colourlessness

experience an abundance of love

she carries with her

slowly steps into the hall

on her rose-petal feet

wears on her an enchanting

everlasting smile

it is an innocent smile of a child

smile of god

she has a mission

a long-lasting mission

to invoke every being

and embrace her divinity

guide the boat ashore safely

in a hall of the congregation

people flocking in

attracted by the charisma

she is a wild bloom

in a tropical forest

born with a lotus posture

came with a smile

did not make any sound

did her penance all through the years

until she was ecstatic with godly love

then one day

one butterfly came

another day betel came

slowly her fragrance spread around the world

many listened to her wisdom

listened to her soulful singing

her disciples came one by one

Once she said

In the end, there is nothing

but a big smile

end of knowledge and beginning of wisdom

with that broad smile, hug and kiss

she hugs and invokes every being and non-being into her
fathomless love

becoming the mother of all mothers

and earth

she made every day a hugging day

by embracing world

Makes you what you are

all of us have worldly sights

wise ones have godly visions

some thoughts come from the depth

others arrive from the head

every day each moment the world blooms

it flowers with a lot of mystery

no one knows what is in store

flower lives a day then retreats

for another moment another day

knowledge and wisdom dawn on some

in a miraculous way

the world is led by a wise shepherd

he foresees the green pastures

leads the sheep rightly

to where he knows the safety

when confronted with blockades

he appears inside and guides

the hindrances are removed

mounting on a mountain

he delivers a sermon

helping us to find the godhead in us

wrapped in a blanket

he carries the calf in his warmth

one day you break the shell

and run to infinity of the world

holding to the rudder of self-confidence

you learn you are a lion

not a goat anymore

the roar from your depth

makes you what you are

Foolish walls

It took generations to build the great wall

many slaves lived there with their fate

toiled dawn to dusk without hopes

became bricks themselves in the buildups

the foundation was laid in the blood and sweat

their children born into the hands of cruel fate

died unknown bodies thrown down the wall

there lies a heap of human bones down unknown unsung

a tragic story is hidden behind every brick laid

tear, blood and sweat flowed down the Huang ho and Yangtze Rivers

every step I climbed was crying loudly of sorrow pain and torture by slave masters

now the so-called human wonder is a pathos song

while Rome was burning Nero was fiddling

so too they are earning foreign exchange

attracting tourists

over time many dynasties ruled

every ruler was slaving their subjects

dictators, autocrats, oligarchy proletarians

they bestowed serfdom on the people

we build many walls among ourselves

psychological, political, geographical

people's freedom is trimmed to a maximum

any sound against the authority is crushed

boots and tanks rolled over the protesters

human history is a story of crushing lives all over the world in
the name of isms and religions

berlin wall, Mexico wall, border walls

human walls of foolish dictators

iron wall,

now we are all closing down against one virus

another wall of nature against cruelty

what is happening to this world

In my dream

Why one needs a body

the fragrance of love blooms

purple jacaranda

can meet you

in my imagination

every day every hour each minute

every nano second

envelop you spiritually

In the arms of a dream

In a world of dreams

In a world of dreams

riding a fantasy of stallions

running a derby

jockeys are nations

fighting each other betting

winning becoming the lead winner

later turn into stakeholders

runs casinos and other corporate houses

captures shares

turns wild attacking all big businesses

owns them

once all the stock exchanges

are controlled they dictate terms

becoming mafia kings of the world

own their finance ministries

formulate economic policies

for the benefit of themselves

try to buy the export business

dumb cheap goods in the world markets

poor nations helped with loans

build roads and bridges dams and ports

then capture the governments with stooges

in short one government of autocrats

sitting under lockdowns

taught us many things

it is time that we all nations of the world

be self-reliant

let us have a united nation based on reality

all the wealth of the nations should belong to

world bank

all nations will be states under the UN

each state head will be a member of the world parliament

one currency, one law, one economy

our future lies in our unification

equal status for all countries

one. community one world

one economy

no trade wars

no world wars

no wars at all

only peace and harmony

a new symphony for the world order

Collector of star dust

At the auspicious time

she gets up as if struck by a falling star

always a dream hanging in her eyes

wipes her sleep away with her hands

seeing on her top of palms as the goddess of wealth

In the middle sits the goddess of learning

lord Vishnu rests at the bottom of her hands

broom lady carries the magic broom to the temple

temple pigeons already started chanting

Vedas in rhythmic hymns slowly

all through there was dancing and drumming

gods goddesses and demigods were singing chanting and
ecstatic dancing, excitement

there were stardusts, sleeping stars and divine flowers

carefully she scooped and swept divine flowers

with meditative steps, she moved around

making the temple sparkling and speckless

had her bath in the temple pond before

receiving the priest with flowers for worship

proudly she walks in quick steps

circumambulating the temple corridor

was erecting step by step to reach the lord

a more deserving divine lady

divine sweeper is a collector of star dust

Dead white flowers

The mighty devil's tree strands spread

a large fortress of green leaves

wild growth across the graveyard

in the late night on a moonless day

mystery waves her black wings

sends her fragrance

of the white bloom

on a dark moonless day

like that, no one dares

to venture out on her way

in the haunted field

there is a beautiful woman

waits near the tree

her black netted

low necked flow gown

voluptuous moons underneath

makes the darkness more attractive
biting her lustful reddish lips is shone
under the dim light of thousands of fireflies
had her robe tastefully decorated
emitting her womanly aroma

beautiful lassi awaits there
biting her lips
chewing her unquenchable desires,
attracted by her charm
men go with her into a comfortable
fairy tree house, she lives

experiencing a tasteful dream
legs moved forward
under the canopy of night snow
hands and body cold,
taking the last puff from the cigarette,
legs trodded carefully
there she was with a charismatic smile
dark wings wave in a state of excitement

took him on her back onto her bed
both in a compromising position
they filled themself in the flood of
passion, lust, emotions, wildly attracted
were eating each other
their lips, bodies finding a place inside them
until dawn, they were fulfilling pruriency
becoming wild cats of fantasy

rooster's clarion she had to return before the first sunlight
one by one bats returned home
hanging upside down on branches

under the sunshine a litter of his nails
and hair curls, cap
fairy's garments were hanging on the branches
scatter of undergarments
dead white flowers
the stale smell of sweat
so goes the myth of a fairy tale

Thirsty dragons

For votive ritual

for oblation fire

spreading slowly

seeping into each cell

vibrant with flames

licking each other

unleashing

clothes, emotions, senses

wild bites of thirsty dragons

He cannot ignore

Lord Vishnu cannot ignore

his devotee in distress

prayers are answered

within no time with a thrust of urgency

he takes incarnation

suitable for the situation

possessing the unique boon

Prahlada's father Hiranyakashipu

was walking tall

was negating every god

and declared himself as god

Lord Vishnu finds a solution

to keep righteousness intact

Prahlada his devotee was

subjected to torture and humiliation

when it was time he arrived

in its fiercest form Narasimha

killed Hiranyakashipu

suspending him in between

earth and sky

sitting on the entrance step

no weapons were used

as per the boon, he killed him with his nails

see his benevolent eye

when Prahlatha prayed

lord came down to peace and harmony

once more

and blessed the world

with his power and grace

here is a fierce god

so simple and loving

gracing every being and non-beings

in the world

the beauty of the Lord Vishnu

is his universal paternal love

flowers of my words

at his holy feet

I worship from the depth of my imagination

petals of peace and harmony

love you, lord,

Mysterious dawn

We were living on a ridge

a cliff house hanging like

cliff hanger, it was a hill station

with underdeveloped town

meagre facilities

we were living in a barn house

a huge granary for paddy,

pepper and coffee beans

children had whale of a time

playing hide and seek

under the storage facility

the winter was very cold

mornings started with a biting breeze

that used to pierce the bones

rarely sun peeped in to wake us up

from the heat of blankets

used to get up at dawn

when those ravens arrive

cleaning, then bluebirds, bulbul

parrots, and pigeons with murmurs

like Brahmin boys chanting Gayathri

bugling water hens

all came to my attention

the hedges and hilltops

bearing the dew pearls

glittering stardusts

blades of grass shining

with globules of mist

fresh bloom flowers hiding

purple bellflowers nodding

shy under a pure white veil

I used to put a pearly drop

from the blade of grass

in my eyes to feel the morning glory

stray dogs hiding

on a sack spread near the steps

often switching his tail

while returning to sleep

my pen stops here

to feel the picture of early morning

So what, her eyes smile

So what, her eyes smile

every cell of her body joins too

in the subtle expression

once she had the cutest of simpering

the most romantic smirk of the renaissance

Davinci lighted her laugh

with lip glow hue

of aesthetics

sculptured her lips with brush strokes

of divine laughter

a masterpiece was born on the canvas

the most adorable allure ever created

viewed by millions and millions

had kept her pulchritude unmasked

coveted, covered in her shyness

in a stream of her dream

Leonard Davinci,

her creator appeared

with a mask on his palette

when he left Monalisa

found her face masked

covering her famous rare laugh

since then all who visited the gallery

was wearing an abstract face cover

she knew the entire world undercover.

A long queue

A long queue line

seems eternal

no one knows who

at the top end

who is at the rear

the sun and moon

rises from the bed

many aeons, the stars

twinkled from time immemorial

men and matters

climbed in the timeline

moved slowly, passed over

disappeared in a mystic mist

although it is conceptual

sometimes it moves as an express train

becomes a slow train often

it slips through the fingers
without any control
no one ever stops it
like a stopwatch, it runs
until the owner
presses stop button

life vanishes
like a dream time too

Another time another world

World passed through
many hurricanes, tornados, tempests
volcanoes erupted
earthquakes, turbulence
high tide revolutions
streaming blood-flooded rivers
hopes sprouted in the veins
of frozen tree trunks

at last, spring came
worthy bloom of thousands
of red roses
it had the smell of sweat and blood
workers and peasants united

proletarian revolution
workers became rulers of the world
laziesfare gave way to das capital

new ideals

Karl Marx Alfred Angel's Stalin, mao tse tung became history

new greed and power equations

one day

a typhoon smashed all

the communist tycoons

proletarian reactionaries in power

renegades survive

It is going to be another

severe monsoon

thunder bolts

Cloudbursts

landslides the entire buildup

shaking

little girl Achilles

on the rampage

we are confined inside homes

trade winds blow severely

one day all will be blown away

be consumed by greed

another time another world

Bouquet of fantasy

our daydreamer just popped

his golden head in the east

with a magic wand

suddenly the field was flooded

with thousands of sun

bright yellow petals

crests at the centre

they node and dance

holding bouquets of crimson rose

they are in love with the golden boy

like a Mexican wave, their heads tilt

just a shake of a magician's baton

the entire field turns into

a forest of little tree plants

with tiny amber bloom

I wipe my eyes in disbelief

Bloodless Revolution

Proudly the tricolour flutters

in the blue sky

symbol of patriotic love for the nation

behind the saffron

the ideal of renunciation for our leaders

white in the centre is light, the path of truth a guide of our conduct

the green shows our relation to the soil

Saffron, White, and Green. Saffron symbolizes courage, bravery, and sacrifice. White represents peace, purity, and truth. Faith, fertility, and prosperity are represented by the Green colour.

I hear the slogans against British

the country all over protests

non-cooperation, strikes, burning of the mill-made clothes, mutiny wearing handspun khadi as prestige

all this was done by a frail man

who guided us through the path of

righteousness, power of nonviolence

the downfall of British looters

started the day when Mahatma

Gandhiji was booted from the train

the most fashionable man from the temple of law, a barrister
was at the receiving end

behind each colour, the people of India united

joined him all the way

suffered, tortured, and many died

executed, words not enough to paint the picture of the
queen's cruelty

still, the British crown

is adorned with the Kohinoor diamond

stolen from India

a symbol of British power?

half-naked fakir taught them the lessons one by one

they had to kneel before him

at last, he did win the battle

for righteous freedom

every inch of the soil of Mother India

resonates the footfalls of that mahatma

and the sacrifice of freedom fighters

vante mathram

Out of blue

Out of the blue one fine thought

splashes skipping to unknown

jumps over the serene lake

rising waves on the surface

settles rolling underneath

it created umpteen chain

of molecular movements

every image reflection was

shaken vibed in turbulence

reforming into shape again

reflects as part of the grandeur

azure complexioned gods

their infinite manifestations

learn to know that you are

a cell in the mighty engineering

the distance between you and him

is just a cobalt dream away

see a lunar reflection just in the lake

floating with soft-feet clouds

wandering in the sapphire

With one touch his smile fades into infinite

the distance of a dream

lives in the depth of sleep

grab the lady of slumber

cover the face in the velvet

you will find gracing visions

one blue moon day

jump out of the ivory tower

you are nothing

but a molecular fantasy

covering the distance

from one cell to another

getting destroyed

into eternity

there nothing is lost

only trekked to

a new generation

wisdom dawns

a secret sacred smile

out of blue

The dark face of the horizon

She was calm, composed serene

smiling like her Barbie doll

suddenly were breathing heavily

nostrils wide, exhaling hot waves

thick blue-black hair fluttering wildly

deep blue eyes rolling like whirlpools

dark bison clouds stampeding around

mountainous oceanic waves of emotion

heaving jumping shouting sea in a tantrum, dark face of the
horizon

Lamps of delight

Everywhere the sound of laughter

the chariot of Truth

driven by horses of the time

emerges from the ocean of darkness

rivers and rivulets flow slowly

carrying the dancing lights

in the mud lamps

streaming magic lights

to the grandeur of ocean mouths

where our forefathers

every city and each village lit with magic lamps of
righteousness

lights of delight

the celebration of victory over demons

happy wide eyes of children,

women in the colourful bests

each cell of the body purified

dances in ecstasy

as sparklers of Diwali

exchanging gifts

sweet packets of love

worshipping the goddess of wealth

every woman becoming sita

men turning into Rama

oh if it was Deepavali every day

Tantrum baby

Some four years back
Mr Frankenstein escaped
from the laboratory
turning the odds
he stepped into the oval
started a frantic freakout
like gold finger
coined slogans for the
desperadoes

all the minimum decency
and etiquette was thrown in the drain
spoken the language of terror
foul mouth spilt salaiva like
street Marshalls and self-styled
sheriff's

threatened world leaders
joined in hands with autocrats
went on holiday with them

he dumped media into dustbins
sacked his ministers very often
took judiciary for a ride
taxed people heavily
but refused to pay his tax
humiliated women
beat them, whipped them

divided people
like an old slave master

he was playing Tom and Jerry
with citizens
unaware the election came
public hit him with a tranquillizer
he is flat on his back
shaking his legs like a tantrum baby

Blue-blooded

last time when Republicans

were sleeping

gold finger occupied the oval office

had his Oddjob with him

his boisterous tongue as

Iron hat to chope off world leaders

all his friends were known

terrorists

he threw his shit

at constitution

mocked at judiciary

like a buffoon

paraded around

with his golf clubs

cheated agreements

challenged world leaders

played and won games
dropping his golf balls

freaked out
in his punk hairstyle
cheated every one
slaved women
taxed people severely
yet he never paid any tax

One day
people dumped him
in the garbage bin
waiting for
the municipality
dump clearers

his only friend
his ego
and blue-blooded
Covid19

The sweetest of all smiles

The sweetest of all smiles

ever lit the earth when he arrived

in the jail of Kamsa was a treasure

cascaded from heaven a full moon

saturated bliss reincarnated in human form

where ever he went the entire world of pulchritude followed

manifestation of cherubic sugary sweetness

dancing with time made his imprint on everyone

flowers bloomed wearing his honeydew

copied the silky soft attire

spread the sandal fragrance of his body

sky copied his skin colour

peacock adorned his crown with quills

elegant music from his celestial flute

intoxicated his worshippers tuning in

With the snap of his fingers, he destroyed

his enemies one by one

eliminated negative characters off the stage

won the war of righteousness

displayed the universal form to the world

flowed Bhagavat Gita directly into the depth of the world

when the time arrived for his departure

he left leaving a honey smile to the people to reminiscent

Snapshot of fireflies

Romantic western sky

golden chariot of the sun just vanished

behind the colourful clouds

the evening just tumbled down from the horizon

from the infinity of light-years

stars slowly winking

the great opera House floodlit

ready for the grand gala opening show

rainbow arch is lit with laser beams

below the nightfalls

street lights high up on the mast

One by one, flat in the skyscrapers

come alive with a sprinkle of sparklings

cars in the full rush with headlights on

like a laser display on a street show

empty cricket ground in the city

slowly angel-winged fireflies arrive

glowing their back

lone angels stepped in

then thousands of them

a synchronised show of aerobic dance

display of flamenco dancers

opera singing

ballet

Kathakali

Bharath Natyam

the whole night the celestial fireworks continue

my pen stops here flabbergasted

Son of God

Entire pulchritude envelopes

around golden aura

saturated concentrated joy

overflowing flooding his compassion

flower petals were strewn on the pathway

a sweet subtle sprinkle of fragrance carries in the intoxicated
breeze

transfixed in a dream sheep follows

the melody of music streams through

joined by a fusion of instruments

exciting breath of the world

anxious to hear his sermons

with one stretch of his feet, he reaches

you and you and you with a feather touch

wipes the pain with a fine caressing

lights a smile on your lips

relieves hunger and poverty by sharing his bread

feeds you with the wine of his blood

while you sleep he waits till you awake

touches by a Quill of his thoughts

guides in your blindness with a stalk

every time he wears a mask

as a father mother, master, brother-sister, and of a poor man
starving

to help you redeem your wealth

encouraging your sacrifice for feeding orphans

he is there a helping hand for all

as master of the universe

son of God, holding you tight in your rope walk above the
towering inferno

Screenplay

The lone papyrus reed
on a mountain cliff
living unnoticed daring
the heat and cold

thundershowers
pricked severely often her body
shaken her hair fluttering
against strong gust

then one day
sun-dried her out
her skin dried basking
she turned into a thin white sheet

breeze took her to the valley
where the Nile was streaming

pure crystal flow

like a meteorite metaphor

she fell in the lap of a saint

reverent took her

and scribbled the first hieroglyphics

he started writing his thoughts

sketching figures conveying

gradually scripts appeared

alphabets started walking

scriptures, epics, Odyssey

writers came alive

William Shakespeare to William Stafford

a whole world of writing

prose, poetry, dramas

a world of letters

literature was born

in every language

my finger is taping

on the keyboard

typing my Imagination

lifting the curtains of my mind

parading leading my muse

to the elegant

screenplay of words

Purity is colourless

a fully bloomed flower

with an exotic colour

the divine poetic hue

spreads aromatic fragrance

the cool breeze carries

it across the continents

fresh thoughts of poetry run

through the veins of his pen

he writes each word

dipping in his blood

dreams of a world of freedom

equality fraternity as humans

he is next to god

far-sighted humble and sees

the future in advance

becoming an Oracle of time

he observes beauty in everything

good bad the ugly all the same

embraces everyone unprejudiced

his muse is colourless purity

his eternal entity

Salabanjïka sculpture

From the mummified annals of time

many brimstone statues of brunettes

they were all walking talking thoughts

lived through the imagination of sculptors

living on the shores of civilization

witnessed turmoils sweeping changes

molten mass boiled in the bowels of the earth

suppressed emotions stoned desires

formed hot lava jumping up and down

by the subtle feather touch of manliness

she rose from the ashes to burning embers

she became a hearth of wild flames

consuming her lover engulfing full

she screamed like lava ablaze

eating everything on the way

she was in a frantic dance

towering over the human entity

she galloped through seasons

ultimately cooling down into pumice stones

soft porous heart full of love

to turn herself into a saalabanjika sculpture

The moon falls into the lake

Contemplating
on a blank canvas
invoked his phantom figures
from heaven

mixed rainbow colours
palette of creativity
meditative horizon
serene silence

suddenly his brushes and bristols
awakens
moves on the horizon
dips into exotically
hued clouds

the painter created her
applied celestial pigments

covered her body
with butterflies
floating on the wings
in suspended animation

fed her
with his lifeblood
breathed life
taught her

my artist walked a few steps
backward
viewed her deeply
judging her from every angle
.

a cool soft subtle breeze
suddenly
lifts off the butterflies

lady covers
her body
with her palms

beauty unveiled

moon falls

In the lake

floating

Springfare lady

As a sapling, she grew up

watching the Godmother forest

she was in a tight corner

where wilderness covered the scenery

sunlight rarely visited

silhouette of giant trunks

forming huge figures consuming

the entire jungle flora

as the sunlight was a rarity

she often climbed the ravine

to peep at the golden boy

feel his rays of excellence

she watched the bushes

around her getting taller and taller

she was reading the jungle book
variety of animal kingdom

wild roaring lions, tigers, wild cats
Wolfs, who always urinate
on her silky attire
trumpeting elephants their stinky dung
deers rabbits, squirrels
colourful rare birds, parrots
in their designer costumes

many seasons walked through
with marching songs
she often talked to the breeze
spoke to animals, tickled rabbits
smelled the fragrance of flowers

peeped at the romantic moon
dancing with stars
watched his reflection
falling in the Rivulet s

unaware she became a young girl

reached puberty

body shaped into adulthood

her texture changed

birds nested in her flew away

fluttering into a new world of freedom.

she dreamed of a memorable spring

turning herself into an elegant maple

her flaming red hair

a soft cascade of pulchritude

my spring fare lady

Dropouts of planets

The kids' dropouts of planets

they moved as asteroid refugees

swimming in a milky way

travelled billions of years

along with comets and meteorites

hardened with time travel

Once collided with earth's extinction

entire species of dinosaurs

burned the entire life forms

the liquid form of bodies frozen

becoming fossils of galaxies as Stonehenge

the great architect time discovered

worked, chiselled out flints

creating masterpiece sculptures

awestruck while my moonlit mind casts a shadow

Dreaming queen

An aroma wades through

sea breeze

the mast is filled with western wind

the mighty barge glides through

Blue Nile waves, an occasional pool

she manoeuvres dancing in elegant steps

her pink steps gleaming

creating a floral pattern on the dance floor

her wide eyes deep blue with love-filled

white robe flutters like the wings of a swan

in the pool white Lillie bloom

spreading the fragrance of Queen Cleo

Mark Antony had left

leaving her in the hands of lonelinesses

her lips still, purple with an ecstatic kiss

tongue relishing the manly tides of the Nile

sighing memories

crushed over evoking desires

unquenchable lust

in the bathhouse, the queen takes a swim

wading through

full bloom lilies and pink lotuses

they sleep in the cradle of sweet memories

she raises her thousand hoods

dark blue hair flashes like a serpent

To an ecstatic dawn

An oceanic depth that takes the vision
deeper and far into a whirlpool fathomless
huge waves of clouds flypast
the unique formation of magical illusion
a visual of forests animals litter of lands
trumpeting elephants, galloping horses
giraffes their long neck designer body
madly running antelopes, monkeys
a whole lot of life forms on parade under
three-ring circus tent.

like a death well motorcyclist
planet Saturn is on the run
moon and stars swing in the trapeze
the azure sky was laden with constellations
dancing planets shooting stars
beaming searchlights
angels visit the circus joining the single-wheel cyclists
they produce stardusts drizzling from the sky

night riders from distant galaxies

the ramp is set with pomp and posh

star queens in their exotic attires

parading on the ring their elegant looks

the breeze caresses the puffy clouds

like a sand artist's quick display of images

Quiet flows the milky way

many celestial beings in swimming trunks

moon takes a plunge from the western horizon

splash of stardusts from heaven

the dance floor was lit

Venus and Jupiter on the floor

lime lighted going round to the tune of divine music

many join the floor with partners

band changes the tune to a quick number

closing eyes

I dived into an unforgettable dream

the world was unfolding before me to an ecstatic dawn

curtain falls

show ends

Bullfight

The grand arena is lit

seats are occupied by the intelligentsia

and prominent citizens.

impatient viewers shouting and whistling

for hot blood

like Dracula

bullfighter arriving in his unique costume

bull already hoofing

bellowing

exposing strong macho muscles

bulges of flesh move rhythmically

as he treads slowly

his red eyes

threatening horns

black sculptured head

brilliance of the sun pours the spotlight

stadium is lit

bright green grass

ring is decorated

ringmaster ready with his uniform

starving bull roars

spreading fear vibes

at last, he comes out in strong steady steps charging Taurus

fighter ready with his muleta

cheering and applauding thirsty viewers

get the beast, kill him

synchronised demand

lust for blood

in the last fight, he was wounded

many arrows struck his neck

blood pouring down

the animal still charging

persistently

his leg falters

head down

a long painful scream of death

crimson neck with streams of blood

at last collapses

like nightfall in the ocean

his blood on the face of the sun

Land of medicine

Hips shaking hippies smoking grass drinking acidic Intellectualism 1

preaching practising Vegetarianism2

often trekking in a psychedelic dream

Psychopharmacology3 inducted

Rememberability 4 fogged in fumes

Policticalization 5 outcasted young men and women, their heart of gold

tested Pyrometallurgical6 investigations

having an Acromonogrammatic 7 aesthetics found no immunopathological 8 disorders and a free Coracoclavicular9 functioning. used Electrodesiccation10 to cure their hypertension and Bilirubinemiac11 is controlled by Ultracrepidarian 12 interventions Unsophisticatedness 13 solves a lot of Evapotranspiration 14 wastes. Demythologisation 15 helps to identify Diagonalizable 16. metamorphosis of life matures into perfection a happy being always

Un word contest

Vegetarianism

Otolaryngologists

Bilirubinemia

Demythologisation

Intellectualism

Hyperbrachycephalic

Pyrometallurgical

Diagonalizable

Astragalotibial

Ultracrepidarian

Psychopharmacology

Acromonogrammatic

Rememberability

Electrodesiccation

Policticalization

Evapotranspiration

Coracoclavicular

Homoeomeria

Unsophisticatedness

Ecstasy

the fragrance of your perfume

seeps into every cell

Violet beads your perspiration

mixed with Yardley silk

your glittering smile

row of Jasmines

into blossom

a breeze whistles

pink clouds touching down

caressing the velvet lavender

they dance intoxicant

opening the stigma and spreading

aromatic ecstasy

eyes fixed wide the lady

watches the infinite purple plants

your lavender hair

teasing my face

let me lie down on your lap

dreaming invoking pruriency

Mother of all

The magnanimous painter

invoked mother nature into her thoughts

she became an elegant Butterfly

her Petal wings gliding in the mist

Blooming, Blossoming with exotic Pigments

the mystic palette had a mixture

of divine shades of colour

with a magic brush, she started painting

in the canvas of her mind

meditative subtle mood

where she had lit a Bonfire

her vision touched everywhere

twisted her dreams like a Kalidoscope

in the Loneliness she invited

white puffy clouds

painted them with matured watercolours

sitting on a Quilt

the painter sketched her self portrait

exhibiting her mother nature

mother of all

Expanding sky

Expanding sky

jumps quiver

to black hole

wry for "z"

Honey Bee lost his stinger

Bulb of an onion

fresh juicy roseate

the bloom of the earth

In petals

she was standing on a solid stem

white flowers

moving dancing with the wind

time climbs up and down

in escalator

the entire universe

travels along

holding to the toothed wheel

every matter transforms

metamorphosis of life

grinding goes on

slowly age captures

rose petals turn pale

wrinkles on skin

oozing blood

stems fall down

decayed foliage

toothless

eventually sheds skin

bones rattle

sturdy corm lacks lustre

one day all the corollas drop

stinky

a purple juice spread

on the soul

each one succumbs

even Mohammed Ali

had a decent

the coloured shaking wings

dropped

honey bee lost his stinger

My complexion

At first, I was scratching

with charcoal on the wall

pumpkin faces

then I got colour pencils

pastels came too

each day became

my canvas

holding bristols of sunlight

I sketched

my abstract complexion

Smile of god

A drop of breast milk on her lips

mother in elated ecstasy

Baby her two fresh milk teeth

her roseate lips opened

like a rosebud bloom

Animals live inside a concrete jungle

just observe people in the go

all well dressed well groomed

manicured pedicured

with a touch of exclusive perfume

in the briefcase hides an action plan

a blueprint for action against

colleagues, subordinates bosses

he or she made up a face mask

there hide many animals and birds

much skeletons in the cupboard

some vultures, ravens and eagles

doves of yesterday's become tigers

ready to pounce at the prey

Wolf's howling loudly at the poor secretary

an elephant stampedes in the office

weeping crocodiles on a colleague's misfortune

roaring lion boss sharpening his nails and fangs

scapegoats black sheep

yellow teethed political thieves

I saw pot-bellied tigers

parade to the tunes of "chenda"

a festival for tigers painted on the big bellies of worshippers

* a festival related to ONAM

Heavenly creation

Those great ladies are in deep sleep

the valley of flowers clangs the girdles

anklets chime as they shift their feet

clear azure sky pulls a canopy over

painted puffy clouds graze idly

exotically coloured cotton candies glide

tweaking birds exhibit their exotic quills

dance to the music of nature

dreaming ladies wake up one by one

a fresh breeze tickles the silk petals

the aromatic fragrance of ladies

spreads in the spring air intoxicated

Golden lotus bloom as golden swans

glide in the crystalline lake of the Himalayas

silver trickling ice beads stream
the valley of flowers opens the gates

the elegant arches of the rainbow
showers of honeydew in the meadows
the great artist sprinkles pigments
pulchritude glides through the ravine
an idyllic extravaganza of the creator

Imagination invents imagery

Imagination invents imagery

involves intelligent images

introduces illusory investment

I initiated installation

into invaluable institutions

Another story another time

My first breath did not reach my lungs

it just disappeared

hands and legs collapsed

I swam away to unknown

after the full stop

the next fresh sentence began

I was in a dream

the world disintegrated

dissolved in the depth of the unknown

the chain of life and death

continues

until the cause and effect

exhausts

now I am wearing a new attire

when it fades

wear and tear takes over

maybe new cloth,

a fresh mask

another life another time

life after life to live and then to die

what happened next

another story of time

Shoot your questions

My pedigree stretched beyond

ranking to 7 generations

now lieutenant colonel on duty

from the academy days

a burly little dog trained in investigation

snooping sniffing detection

deception combating identification

narcotics what not

Mom and Dad were detectives

thief capturers

firefighters' night watchdogs

their discipline made a dare-devil out of me

the mission now is to sniff

to the hideout of terrorists

side by side I can smell and capture

skunk and sneaky mongoose

See my gallantry awards on

neck collar for distinctive services

usually, I avoid publicity

no media exclusives

I take one question from each scribe

Please shoot your questions

Where is colour

Elevated the aeroplane floated

it moved up and up among clouds

a calm space leaving behind

the Altostratus clouds Altocumulus clouds Stratus clouds,
Stratocumulus clouds

now a vast plain of the magnificent sky

an eternal azure ocean

ripple less waveless stratosphere

the giant airbus left underneath a big dramatic world of names
and forms

lies there a big world

tinned

magic of enlightenment

everything in the world became Lilliputians

up in the heights of magnanimity

there is nothing that exists except

a wild embrace of loving hands

bound together

everything vanished in the thin air

no colour creed religious relationship

do you know you are a nano micro dust

at the feet of universal magnitude

shall be assimilated by the time

where does the colour stand

Sir Isaac Newton's colour disc displays

no pigments

Fairyland

Before our eyes, a fairyland was unfolding

In the valley of the Alps

sandwiched between Swiss and Austria

our tour guide declared

we will be spending one hour on this

tiny little alpine country capital Vaduz

with a jerk the Polish driver

parked our bus in the heart of the city centre

on the hilltop

the ruler's castle was waking up

from the winter blanket of snow

a golden glint of sunlight spreads

people queued at the shopping mall

a colourful ridable miniature rail took us around the town

as a souvenir, I got my passport stamped entry and exited at
the counter

for two euros.

the richest nation with a high GDP
still, cuddling under the blanket
we left the country before the dawn
sets her feet in the fairyland

[when the small I crossed big I]

When the small I crossed big I

Jesus Christ was born in the heart

resurrected in each core

For 'that' smile

At this evening hour

a small window opened to the beautiful dawn I had once, we
all had

that day, I remember the first breath

I took with mother's help

then on to this rattling age

years and years of fall

how many helping hands

helped, carried cared

built this body up.

known and unknown men, women

birds, animals and bacteria

filled every wish

then oared rowed the boat this far

there was a hand of providence

pushed and pulled me out
of situations

bow down to that magnanimity
with a beaming smile
a prayer to all, salutations
thank you universe thank you
kindly help me cross across
to the shore of immortality
for that eternal smile of bliss

Golden deluge

Silhouetted giant coconut trees

heads nod like excited peacocks

their long greenish-blue quills

the dance continues until moonlit fades

the ocean waves weave a cobalt silk carpet

glitter of decorative stardust

moon takes a deep sigh and releases minuscule droplets of
water

like a golden deluge the ocean rolls

the seashells glitter under moonlit like diamonds

far away from the howl of a stray dog

the tide is forming in the backwaters

my shortened shadow steps behind me

fireflies dance the palm trees

making wonderful designs in the air

a flash of a fish spilling golden grains

Bliss

Young and old sit around him

the banyan tree

leaves shake in ecstasy

a cool breeze

singing bluebirds

ripe little fruits fall

blue moonlit

drizzles

cover the earth

the master sits in silence

neither questions

nor answers

their entity is lost

at the feet of the guru

silence conveys

students satisfied

they dive deep into bliss

From the first breath onwards

The lone Palmyra tree

stands watching the sky theatre

birds retreat in clusters

synchronized gliding against the dusk sky

the sun shows his wrinkled face

once again through the grey sky before the sky fall

a litter of smashed clouds move fast

soon the swords of darkness will swing

evenings were colourful

the great sand artists were sketching

sprayed exotic colours

created live images on the horizon

our evenings were lively

found the angels floating

dolphins diving from the cobalt sea

ecstatic mermaids dancing

found their hands raised

blessings unconditionally

all through this life

from the first breath

till this evening

they were inhaling and exhaling

fed, cared for, and sang lullabies

guided with the hands of Providence

universe thank you

all the blessings, guidance, abundance,

great health, miracles, love, safety

that I already have

and I am receiving abundantly today

and for ways to help and contribute to others

thank you from my heart

The allure of the night

Spilt obsidian night

the darkness seeps slowly

her black complexion

embossed against

the frame of a white silky robe

curved figure jasmine teeth

her diamond nosering

beaming lighthouse

allure of night

Magician of the universe

Scintillating flute music
channelling through the valley
Crystal water flows through Yamuna
grazing cows their dark wide eyes
bathing gopikas
the intoxicating smell of sandal paste.

silent serenity
imagery of pareekshith
little Krishna
his unique azure divine colour
little crown small earrings
elegant waist chain
anklets diamond bangles
kousthuba

the swish of yellow silk
a moving flute

nodding peacock quills

a cascade of blueish dark clouds

two feet moving

soft silent footfall

the imprint of lotus feet

smiling blooms

fragrance of basil

yes he is near

pure butter balls move in the air

yes he is born

in every heart

magician of the universe

To the world

Each petal spun

with delicate silk chromosomes

drawn from the depth of the mother

tinted purple soft petals

as the day is born

with crimson halo

the daydreamer

holds a pinkish beam

a bouquet of pink roses

to the world

Am I right?

the entire earth floats

just hangs

turns like baubles

glass balls

little globules afloat
in the galaxy of space

tiny planets
dance in precision
and in the magnum opus
of Milkyway

the land mass floats
in the oceanic waves
precariously levitate
like seven pieces of pizza
seasoned with
rivers mount mountains
trees forests
fixed tight to mud

yet a tsunamic wave
shakes
consumes
sweeps Shadow's

earthquakes

silhouetted with a giant shadow

yes we little birds

rests take a nap

owning the shadow

am I right?

Dawn in her

The aesthetic

sculpture of the sun

holds the colour

she embraced

magnificent

pulchritude

of dawn

in her bosom

Dame nature

dame nature

incarnated

bathed in elegance

consecrated

in the purity of torrent

turned

a live statue

of universe

Pretty dimples

He just invoked her through flute holes

with the sweetest of ragas from his lips

Radha floated on his roseate lips dancing

ambrosia of their love percolated in the universe

birds animal trees, everything on earth

became idols and images of RadheKridhna

continuous glow and flow of celestial music

when Radha chanted Krishna the whole of creation answered

the breeze carried the aroma of love

thoughts winged as butterflies in sky blue

the sun had the face of the lord with a sandal mark on the
forehead

had the cool smile playing music

the sky adopted his soft azure hue

dark clouds wore his long hair

stars and planets formed his ornaments

Sun his charioteer driving through

Radha the beautiful reflective music of his platonic love with
pretty dimples

Food for thoughts

Just listen to a painful helpless shriek
from the depth of the deep freezer
mechanised civilized guillotined heads
systematic killings for steak whatever

someone lost his life by a strong hit
with a hammer food for thoughts?

Jigsaw puzzle

Sat there how long

I don't know

the lone beach bench

technicolour horizon

dawn sun

just rose from

the eastern sea

I was solving a jigsaw

Black hole geode

A nebulous recollection

I was cruising in a dream

In the Milkyway

it is stuffed with galaxies

stars twinkling studded with

cobwebs of mighty constellations

innumerable Suns dead stars

arteries veins and capillaries

of the mysterious universe

black hole geode